Editor
Eric Migliaccio

Illustrator
Mark Mason

Cover Artist
Brenda DiAntonis

Editor in Chief
Ina Massler Levin, M.A.

Creative Director
Karen J. Goldfluss, M.S. Ed.

Art Production Manager
Kevin Barnes

Art Coordinator
Renée Christine Yates

Imaging
Rosa C. See

Publisher
Mary D. Smith, M.S. Ed.

Content Area Lessons Using **Graphic Organizers** — Grade 4

- Teach content and thought processes simultaneously
- Promote inferential and evaluative thinking
- Improve critical and analytical thinking skills
- Enhance cross-curricular understandings

CD-ROM

Teacher Created Resources

Author

Debra J. Housel, M.S. Ed.

Teacher Created Resources, Inc.
6421 Industry Way
Westminster, CA 92683
www.teachercreated.com

ISBN: 978-1-4206-8094-2

© 2008 Teacher Created Resources, Inc.
Made in U.S.A.

Teacher Created Resources

Table of Contents

Introduction

Content Area Lessons Using Graphic Organizers is designed to save you time and effort. It contains complete lessons that meet the standards for your grade level in reading, writing, science, geography, history, and math. Each lesson uses a different graphic organizer. Thus, if you do all the lessons in this book and never use another graphic organizer, your students will have worked with 23 different graphic organizers. This provides significant exposure to these important educational tools.

Graphic organizers show the organization of concepts and the relationships among them. They offer a clear depiction of data, which research has proven is more memorable than pages of notes. They show students "how it all fits together," which is much more effective than having them try to memorize bits of data without thoroughly understanding the context. Showing how information is organized helps students—especially English-language learners and those with reading disabilities—focus on content instead of semantics and grammar.

Compelling Reasons to Use Graphic Organizers

Research shows that graphic organizers actually improve students' creative, analytical, and critical-thinking skills. Why? Graphic organizers help students of all ages to process information. Processing information is a complex skill requiring the ability to identify essential ideas; decide which details are relevant and which are irrelevant; understand how information is structured; and perhaps most importantly of all, figure out how data relates to other information or situations. Processing information demands the use of such higher-level thinking skills as making decisions, drawing conclusions, and forming inferences.

Substantial amounts of research support the fact that graphic organizers increase the understanding and retention of critical information for students who range from gifted to those with learning disabilities. This means that using graphic organizers may meet the needs of the many different learners in your classroom without the time-consuming task of individualization.

The visual element inherent in graphic organizers supports three cognitive-learning theories: dual coding theory, schema theory, and cognitive load theory.

- **Dual coding theory** acknowledges that presenting information in both visual and verbal form improves recall and recognition. Graphic organizers do both effectively.

- **Schema theory** states that a learner's prediction based on his or her background knowledge (schema) is crucial for acquiring new information. This is why readers have a hard time comprehending material in an unfamiliar subject even when they know the meaning of the separate words in the text. Graphic organizers' ability to show relationships builds upon and increases students' schema.

- **Cognitive load theory** stresses that a student's short-term memory has limitations in the amount of data it can simultaneously hold. Since any instructional information must first be processed by short-term memory, for long-term memory (schema acquisition) to occur, instruction must reduce the short-term memory load. Thus, teaching methods that cut down on the demands of short-term memory give the brain a better opportunity to facilitate activation of long-term memory. Graphic organizers fit the bill perfectly.

Graphic organizers are appearing more often in standardized tests and state assessments. Giving your students practice with the variety of graphic organizers offered in this book can help them to achieve better scores on these assessments.

Introduction *(cont.)*

How to Use This Book

Each lesson in *Content Area Lessons Using Graphic Organizers* is designed to be used where it fits into your curriculum. Whenever you start a new unit, check to see if one of these lessons will work with your topic. Where applicable, reading levels based on the Flesch-Kincaid formula are included.

The lessons often require that you make a transparency and student copies of the graphic organizers located on the CD. Any other necessary materials will be stated in the lesson. These might include such things as highlighters, index cards, poster board, scissors, glue, and zipper bags. If possible, when writing on the overhead transparency, use different colors to differentiate between specific sections. This is another way to help your students to visualize data.

The graphic organizers give as much space as possible for the students to write. However, if some of your students have large handwriting, make an overhead transparency of the blank graphic organizer and display it on the overhead. Then have a school aide or the students tape a sheet of construction paper where the overhead projects and copy the format onto the paper. This will give them more room to write.

If you are just starting to use graphic organizers, you may worry that they are time-consuming. Keep in mind that it is time well spent. Graphic organizers provide meaningful instruction that gives your students an advantage in comprehending and remembering data. By using graphic organizers you are teaching not just content but thought processes. Your students are learning how to learn—an invaluable skill that will serve them well for the rest of their lives.

Be Flexible and Creative

The graphic organizers included in *Content Area Lessons Using Graphic Organizers* have many uses; they are not limited to the lessons or subject area in which they appear. Most of these graphic organizers can be used or modified to fit the needs of other lessons or subjects. Sometimes a student will self-advocate by asking you to make copies of a certain kind for use in other areas. You may find that a challenged student enjoys and learns best using one particular type. Be flexible and creative in your use of graphic organizers.

If you have a class that really enjoys graphic organizers, you could opt to evaluate student learning by letting the students create their own graphic organizers. You may be pleasantly surprised by your students' abilities to make meaningful graphics that show interrelationships in a more effective way than they could explain in writing.

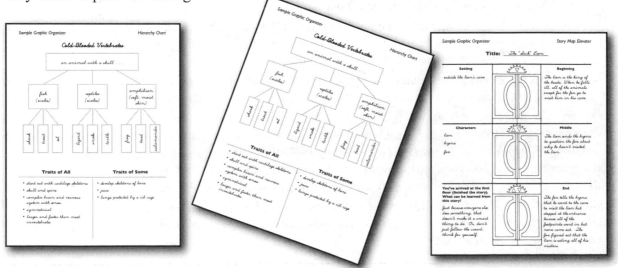

Standards Correlation Chart

Each lesson in this book meets at least one of the following standards and benchmarks, which are used with permission from McREL.

Copyright 2006 McREL. Mid-continent Research for Education and Learning
2250 S. Parker Road, Suite 500. Aurora, CO 80014
Telephone: 303-337-0990. Website: *www.mcrel.org/standards-benchmarks*

Standards and Benchmarks	Pages
Math	
Standard 2. Understands and applies basic and advanced properties of the concepts of numbers	
• **Benchmark 2.** Understands equivalent forms of basic percents, fractions, and decimal, and when one form of a number might be more useful than another	14–16
• **Benchmark 5.** Understands the relative magnitude and relationships among whole numbers, fractions, decimals, and mixed numbers	14–16
Standard 3. Uses basic and advanced procedures while performing the processes of computation	
• **Benchmark 1.** Adds, subtracts, multiplies, and divides whole numbers and decimals	11–13
• **Benchmark 7.** Solves real-world problems involving number operations (e.g., computations with dollars and cents)	8–10, 11–13
History	
Standard 2. Understands the history of a local community and how communities in North America varied long ago	
• **Benchmark 2.** Knows geographical settings, economic activities, food, clothing, homes, crafts, and rituals of Native American societies long ago (e.g., Iroquois, Sioux, Hopi, Nez Perce, Inuit, Cherokee)	17–20
Standard 3. Understands the people, events, problems and ideas that were significant in creating the history of their states	
• **Benchmark 2.** Understands geographic, economic, and religious reasons that brought the first explorers and settlers to the state or region, who they were, and where they settled	29–33
Standard 4. Understands how democratic values came to be, and how they have been exemplified by people, events, and symbols	
• **Benchmark 3.** Understands how people over the last 200 years have continued to struggle to bring to all groups in American society the liberties and equality promised in the basic principles of American democracy	25–28
• **Benchmark 6.** Understands historical figures who believed in the fundamental democratic values and the significance of these people both in their historical context and today	25–28
• **Benchmark 11.** Understands how songs, symbols, and slogans demonstrate freedom of expression and the role of protest in a democracy	25–28
Standard 6. Understands the folklore and other cultural contributions from various regions of the United States and how they helped to form a national heritage	
• **Benchmark 2.** Understands how stories, legends, songs, ballads, games, and tall tales describe the environment, lifestyles, beliefs, and struggles of people in various regions of the country	21–24

Standards Correlation Chart *(cont.)*

Standards and Benchmarks	Pages
Geography	
Standard 1. Understands the characteristics and uses of maps, globes, and other geographic tools and technologies	
• **Benchmark 1.** Knows the basic elements of maps and globes	31, 34–36
Standard 2. Knows the location of places, geographic features, and patterns of the environment	
• **Benchmark 1.** Knows major physical and human features of places as they are represented on maps and globes (e.g., large cities, rivers, mountains, locations of places discussed in history, etc.)	31, 34–36
• **Benchmark 2. Knows** the location of major cities in North America	31, 34–36
Standard 7. Knows the physical processes that shape patterns on Earth's surface	
• **Benchmark 2.** Understands how physical processes help to shape features and patterns on Earth's surface	49–52
Standard 8. Understands the characteristics of ecosystems on Earth's surface	
• **Benchmark 2.** Knows ways in which humans can change ecosystems	41–44
Standard 15. Understands how physical systems affect human systems	
• **Benchmark 4.** Knows natural hazards that occur in the physical environment, including floods, hurricanes, tornadoes, and earthquakes	45–48
Standard 16. Understands the changes that occur in the meaning, use, distribution, and importance of resources	
• **Benchmark 5.** Knows the advantages and disadvantages of recycling and reusing different types of materials	37–40
Standard 18. Understands global development and environmental issues	
• **Benchmark 2.** Knows the ways in which resources can be managed and why it is important to do so	37–40
Science	
Standard 2. Understands Earth's composition and structure	
• **Benchmark 1.** Knows how features on Earth's surface are constantly changed by a combination of slow and rapid processes (e.g., erosion, landslides, volcanic eruptions, earthquakes, etc.)	49–52
• **Benchmark 3.** Knows that rock is composed of different combinations of minerals	49–52
Standard 5. Understands the structure and function of cells and organisms	
• **Benchmark 1.** Knows that plants and animals progress through life cycles of birth, growth, and development, reproduction, and death; the details of these life cycles are different for different organisms	61–64
• **Benchmark 3.** Knows that the behavior of individual organisms is influenced by internal cues (e.g., hunger) and external cues (e.g., changes in the environment) and that humans and other organisms have senses that help them to detect these cues	57–64
Standard 6. Understands relationships among organisms and their physical environment	
• **Benchmark 3.** Knows that an organism's patterns of behavior are related to the nature of that organism's environment	57–64
Standard 7. Understands biological evolution and the diversity of life	
• **Benchmark 2.** Knows different ways in which living things can be grouped and purpose of different groupings	57–60
Standard 10. Understands forces and motion	
• **Benchmark 1.** Knows that magnets attract and repel each other and attract certain kinds of other materials	53–56
Standard 13. Understands the scientific enterprise	
• **Benchmark 2.** Knows that although people using scientific inquiry have learned much about the objects, events, and phenomena in nature, science is an ongoing process and will never be finished	49–52

Standards Correlation Chart *(cont.)*

Standards and Benchmarks	Pages
Language Arts	
Standard 1. Uses the general skills and strategies of the writing process	
• **Benchmark 1.** Uses prewriting strategies to plan written work (e.g., uses graphic organizers; groups related ideas; organizes information)	65–68, 73–76, 85
• **Benchmark 2.** Uses strategies to draft and revise written work	73–76, 85
• **Benchmark 3.** Uses strategies to edit and publish written work	73–76, 85
• **Benchmark 4.** Evaluates own and others' writing	77–80, 85
• **Benchmark 6.** Uses strategies to write for a variety of purposes (e.g. to inform, entertain, explain, describe, record ideas)	65–68, 73–76, 85
• **Benchmark 9.** Writes autobiographical compositions	73–76
Standard 3. Uses grammatical and mechanical conventions in written compositions	
• **Benchmark 4.** Uses nouns in written compositions	73–80
• **Benchmark 5.** Uses verbs in written compositions	77–80
• **Benchmark 6.** Uses adjectives in written compositions	69–72, 77–80
• **Benchmark 7.** Uses adverbs in written compositions	77–80
• **Benchmark 10.** Uses conventions of spelling in written compositions (e.g., uses compounds, roots, suffixes, prefixes, and syllable constructions to spell words)	69–72
Standard 4. Gathers and uses information for research purposes	
• **Benchmark 8.** Uses strategies to compile information into written reports or summaries (e.g., incorporates notes into finished product; includes simple facts, details, explanation and examples, etc.; uses appropriate visual aids)	65–68
Standard 5. Uses the general skills and strategies of the reading process	
• **Benchmark 3.** Represents concrete information (e.g., persons, places, things, and events) as explicit mental pictures	81–84
• **Benchmark 5.** Uses phonetic and structural analysis techniques, syntactic structure and semantic context to decode unknown words	89–93
• **Benchmark 8.** Understands level-appropriate reading vocabulary	89–93
• **Benchmark 11.** Understands the author's purpose	37, 94–96
Standard 6. Uses reading skills and strategies to understand and interpret a variety of literary texts	
• **Benchmark 1.** Uses reading skills and strategies to understand a variety of literary passages and texts (e.g., fables, poems, fairy tales, etc.)	65–68, 73–76 81–88
• **Benchmark 2.** Knows the defining characteristics of a variety of literary forms and genres	77–84
• **Benchmark 3.** Understands the basic concept of plot	94–96

Day 1

1. Prior to this lesson, your students must know the value of coins (10 nickels equals 50 cents, or half a dollar is 50 cents), be able to identify odd and even numbers, and do multiplication and division.

2. Make an overhead transparency and copies of the "Laying Tiles" graphic organizer on page 10. Obtain clear number tiles (or cut out the ones on your transparency) to use on the overhead.

3. Have your students cut out the individual number tiles on the page.

4. Have your students glue their tile boards to pieces of poster board and store their number tiles in a zipper bag.

5. Say, "We are going to use each tile once. Place the tiles moving from top to bottom. I will ask a question about money, and you will place the tiles. Do not shout out the answer. If you don't know one, skip it. We'll go over it." Repeat each question twice. Be sure to point out the appropriate spot for them to place their tiles on the graphic organizer and give enough time for students to think.

6. Ask these questions: What is the value of a quarter? (*25¢*) What is half of 34 cents? (*17¢*) What is the value of 3 dimes? (*30¢*) What is twice the value of 43 cents? (*86¢*) I have 7 groups of 7 pennies. How much do I have in all? (*49¢*)

7. Go over the answers, asking individual students to explain how they determined the right answer. Have the students clear their boards.

8. Repeat the procedure. This time have students work independently, having a student come up and display the correct answers on the overhead afterwards. Ask these questions: What's the value of three quarters? (*75¢*) If 63 cents is split among three friends, how much does each get? (*21¢*) What's the value of 3 dozen pennies? (*36¢*) I have 79 cents and find a dime. How much do I have in all? (*89¢*) What's the value of 8 nickels? (*40¢*)

Days 2–5

1. Have students get out their tile boards and number tiles.

2. Repeat the activity above using a variety of money questions you have prepared in advance.

Next Week

1. Have students get out their tile boards and number tiles.

2. Pair the students. They must place all 10 digits in any order and then write appropriate money questions next to each number. This is challenging because the children must generate the questions and can use each digit only once.

3. Have the pair write their number sentences and answers on a piece of paper to turn in.

4. If your class enjoys this activity, you can eventually have them do it independently.

Note: This is filled in with the answers to the set of clues given in #6 on page 8.

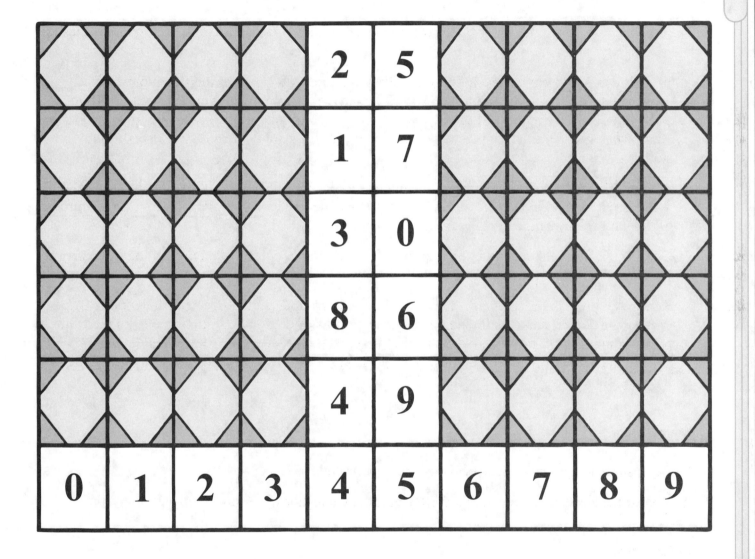

Math

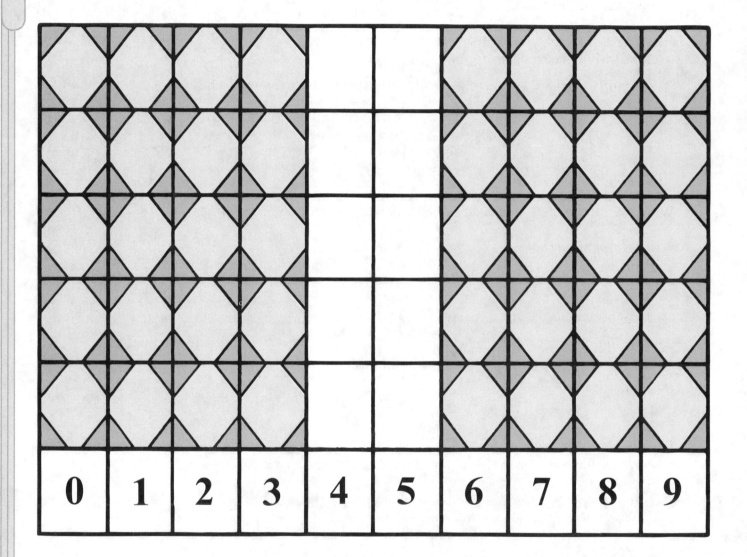

| 0 | 1 | 2 | 3 | 4 | 5 | 6 | 7 | 8 | 9 |

1. Prior to this lesson, your students must be familiar with addition and subtraction of decimals with regrouping.

2. Make an overhead transparency and copies of the "Follow the Steps" graphic organizer on page 13.

3. Write this word problem at the top of your transparency:

> *Kwan ran the 300-yard dash in 93.2 seconds. Daryl ran it in 86.5 seconds. How much faster was Daryl's time?*

4. Working as a whole class, solve the problem step by step, filling in the transparency on the overhead while the students do so at their seats.

   - *Identify:* Kwan's time is 93.2 sec; Daryl's time is 86.5. How much faster?
   - *Decide:* "How much faster" gives a clue. It means to compare. So, we will subtract.
      93.2 – 86.5 = how many seconds faster
   - *Solve:* 93.2 – 86.5 = 6.7 seconds
   - *Check:* 6.7 + 86.5 = 93.2 seconds

5. Wipe the transparency clean and solve this problem as a class, as well:

> *To get from Pinehurst to Toadstool, you must take three roads. A map shows the length of these roads. One is 13.9 miles long, the next is 28.4 miles long, and the third is 87 miles long. How many miles must you drive to get from Toadstool to Pinehurst?*

   - *Identify:* Need to take three roads: 13.9, 28.4, and 87 miles. How many miles?
   - *Decide:* Want the distance between the places. Must add the length of the roads.
      13.9 + 28.4 + 87.0 = number of miles
   - *Solve:* 13.9 + 28.4 + 87.0 = 129.3 miles
   - *Check:* 129.3 – 13.9 – 28.4 – 87 = 0

6. Distribute another copy of the "Follow the Steps" graphic organizer to students. Write this problem on the board or overhead and have the students do it independently:

> *Lara needs 3.75 yards of cloth to make a costume. She also needs 1.8 yards of cloth to make a hat. How much cloth must she buy in all?*

   - *Identify:* 3.75 yd for costume and 1.8 yd for hat. How much in all?
   - *Decide:* "How much in all" gives a clue. It means to find a total. So, we will add.
      3.75 + 1.8 = total yards of cloth
   - *Solve:* 3.75 + 1.8 = 5.55 yards
   - *Check:* 5.55 - 1.8 = 3.75 yards OR 5.55 - 3.75= 1.8 yards

7. Use this graphic organizer for each word problem the students do until they have the steps memorized.

Note: The "Follow the Steps" graphic organizer can be used as a sequencing organizer in any subject area if you cover the words on the steps and in the boxes before you make copies.

Sample Graphic Organizer   *Follow the Steps*

Note: This is filled in with the example in #6 from page 11.

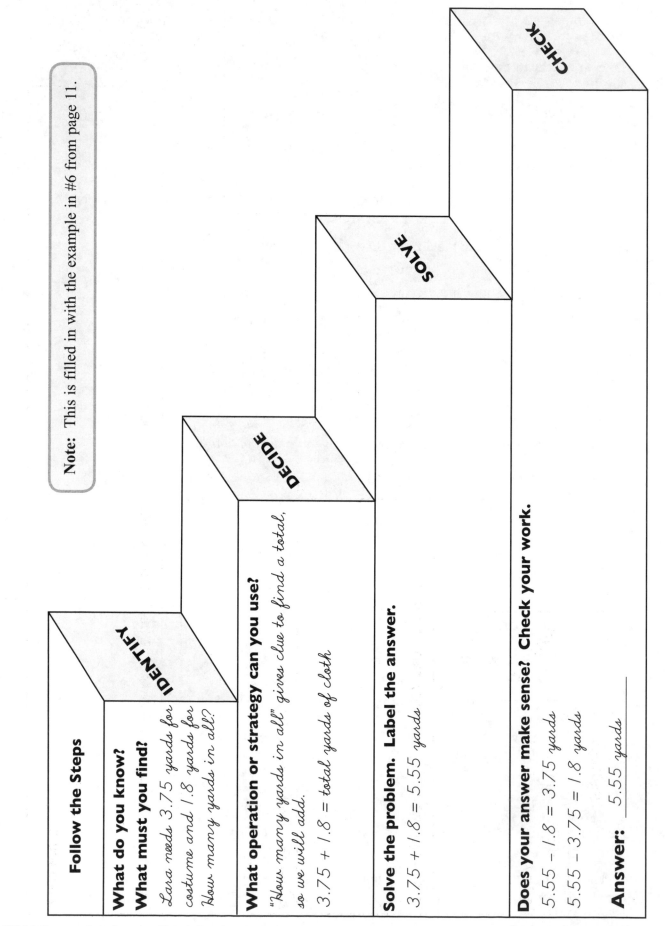

Follow the Steps

What do you know?
What must you find?

Lara needs 3.75 yards for costume and 1.8 yards for. How many yards in all?

What operation or strategy can you use?

"How many yards in all" gives clue to find a total, so we will add.

3.75 + 1.8 = total yards of cloth

Solve the problem. Label the answer.

3.75 + 1.8 = 5.55 yards

Does your answer make sense? Check your work.

5.55 – 1.8 = 3.75 yards
5.55 – 3.75 = 1.8 yards

Answer: _5.55 yards_

IDENTIFY

DECIDE

SOLVE

CHECK

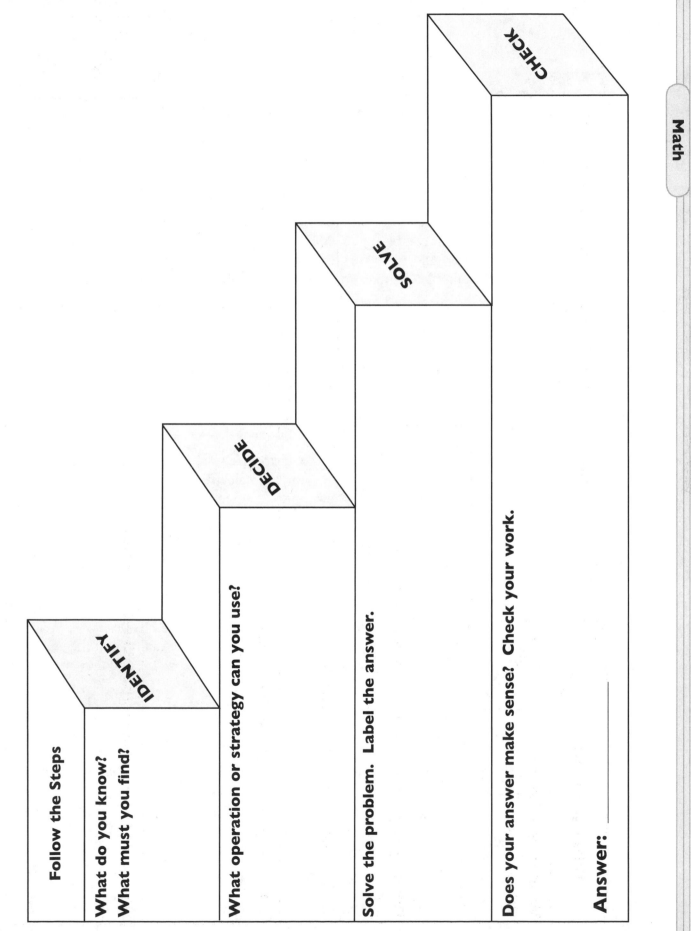

Follow the Steps

**What do you know?
What must you find?**

IDENTIFY

What operation or strategy can you use?

DECIDE

Solve the problem. Label the answer.

SOLVE

Does your answer make sense? Check your work.

CHECK

Answer: _____

Math

Day 1

1. Prior to doing this lesson, your students should be familiar with fractions, improper fractions, mixed numbers, ratios, decimals, and money. This lesson is intended to solidify your students' understanding of how numbers are related and expressed—for example, that $^3/_6$ is the same as $^1/_2$ and can also be expressed as .5.

2. Make an overhead transparency and student copies of the "It's All Relative" graphic organizer on page 16.

3. Distribute the copies and display the transparency. Write ".05" in the "Expression" column while the students do so at their seats. Ask the students to explain what it means (5 out of 100) and another way in which it can be expressed ($^5/_{100}$). Challenge them to come up with a real-life example. One is provided for you in the completed graphic organizer on page 15. You can offer the information in the completed graphic organizer whenever your class is stumped.

4. For the second row, write "42 cents out of 100 cents in a dollar" in the "What It Means" column. Have the students provide the information for the rest of the columns.

5. For the third row, write "the ratio of 7 to 8" in the "What It Means" column and ask the students to volunteer the information for the rest of the columns in the row. This is a great opportunity to reinforce the fact that ratios are basically a different way of writing a fraction.

6. In the fourth row, write "The shirt only had $^3/_8$ of its buttons" in the "Real-Life Example" column and ask the students to volunteer the information for the rest of the columns in the row.

7. For the fifth row, write "$1^8/_9$" in the "Can Also Be Expressed As" column. Guide your students to fill in the rest of the columns. Be sure to take time to clear up misconceptions that you may discover when the students volunteer answers.

8. For the sixth row, write, "There were four pizzas cut into five slices each, and the kids at the party ate $5^2/_5$ of the pizzas" in the "Real-Life Example" column. Ask your students to tell you how much pizza is left (three slices). Then ask how to fill in the first two columns. Show your students how to convert a mixed number to a decimal.

9. For the seventh row, tell your students, "A tenth of a penny is called a mill. A mill is used when determining tax, especially tax on a gallon of gas or on property value or sales tax." Write "The tax rate is 89 one thousandths" in the "Real-Life Example" column. See if the students can supply the information for the remaining columns. This one is tricky, and they may need guidance.

Day 2

1. Write these words on the board or overhead projector: *fractions, improper fractions, mixed numbers, ratios, decimals,* and *money.*

2. Pair students and distribute another copy of the graphic organizer to them.

3. Have them generate seven numbers that they can explain, express in another way, and come up with a real-world example for. This will be challenging, so pair stronger math students with weaker ones. Do not expect the variety that you provided them.

Note: The "It's All Relative" graphic organizer can also be used with science or language arts.

Math

Expression	What It Means	Can Also Be Expressed As	Real-Life Example
.05	5 divided by 100	$\frac{5}{100}$	5% of the students forgot to do their math assignment.
$0.42	42 cents out of 100 cents in a dollar	$\frac{42}{100}$ or 42¢	I need $0.42 more in order to afford the box of candy.
7:8	a ratio of 7 to 8	$\frac{7}{8}$ .875	The ratio of boys to girls in Mr. Smith's class is 7 to 8. There are 14 boys and 16 girls.
$\frac{3}{8}$	three-eighths (3 parts of a thing cut into 8 parts)	.375	The shirt only had $\frac{3}{8}$ of its buttons (5 were missing).
$\frac{17}{9}$	improper number (17 of a thing split into 9 parts)	$1\frac{8}{9}$	There are two pans of brownies, with 9 brownies in each pan. Someone ate just one of the brownies, so there are $\frac{17}{9}$ left (or 1 full pan and $\frac{8}{9}$ of the second pan).
$5\frac{2}{5}$	5 wholes and 2 of 5 parts	5.4	There were six pizzas cut into five slices each, and the kids at the party ate $5\frac{2}{5}$ of the pizzas (three pieces are left).
$\frac{89}{1000}$	89 divided by 1,000	.089	The tax rate is 89 one thousandths (also called 8.9%).

Math

Expression	What It Means	Can Also Be Expressed As	Real-Life Example

Day 1

1. This would be a good introduction to a unit about the Inuit. Before doing this lesson, have available books, encyclopedias, access to the Internet, and other reference materials for students to investigate this group of people.

2. Make and distribute copies of the poem "The Kayak" on page 18.

3. Make an overhead transparency and student copies of the "K-W-L Chart" organizer on page 20.

4. Write the vocabulary words on the board. See if your students know the definition of any of them. Provide the definitions for any they do not know.

   ❖ **kayak** (KI-yak)—an Inuit canoe with a skin covering over a light framework, made watertight by a flexible closure around the waist of the occupant and propelled with a double-bladed paddle

   ❖ **briny**—salty

   ❖ **Eskimo**—old-fashioned word used for the Inuit, the native tribes that live in the Arctic Circle, which includes parts of North America, Greenland, and Siberia (a region in Asia)

   ❖ **billows**—great waves

   ❖ **skiff**—a one-person boat moved by oars

   ❖ **lance**—a long stick with a pointed end used as a hunting weapon

   ❖ **trim**—lighten the load

5. Have individual students read aloud each stanza of "The Kayak."

6. Distribute student copies and display the overhead transparency of the graphic organizer.

7. Ask your students what they know about the Inuit from reading the poem. Use the information to fill in the first column.

8. Ask students what they wonder about the Inuit. Write at least four of their questions on the transparency. Each member of the class has the choice to research those questions or questions of their choice (as long as four questions are researched). Explain that they are to write the answers in the third column of the graphic organizer.

Days 2–3

1. Give your students time to investigate the books and other materials you gathered prior to the lesson. Depending on the complexity of the questions, you may need to give them time over several days.

2. Create a large K-W-L chart on a piece of poster board. List the questions posed by the class (from the transparency).

3. Reconvene as a whole group. Ask volunteers to provide the answers and write them across from the questions on the K-W-L. Have students who pursued their own questions offer what they learned and add it to the class chart. Keep the class K-W-L chart on display throughout the unit.

History

The Kayak

Over the briny waves I go,

In spite of the weather, in spite of the snow.

What cares the hardy Eskimo?

In my little skiff, with paddle and lance,

I glide where the foaming billows dance.

'Round me the sea birds dip and soar;

Like me, they love the ocean's roar.

Sometimes a floating iceberg gleams

Above me with its melting streams.

Sometimes a rushing wave will fall

Down on my skiff and cover it all.

But what care I for a wave's attack?

With my paddle I right my little kayak

And then its weight I speedily trim,

And over the water away I skim.

History

K-W-L Chart

I Know	I Wonder	I Learned
Inuit were called Eskimos	What did they hunt with the lance and kayak?	They hunted whales and seals.
used kayaks (single-person boat) on ocean	What did they wear to stay warm?	They wore sealskin clothes. They wore two layers—one with the fur facing toward their bodies and one with the fur facing away.
snow and floating icebergs (cold habitat)	What were their homes like?	Most of the time they lived in sod and rock houses (domes); while they were hunting, they built ice houses (igloos) on the shore.
used weapon called a lance	What were their kayaks made of?	Their kayaks were made of sealskin.
	How did they waterproof their kayaks?	Each year they coated their kayaks with whale blubber to make them waterproof.
	Was it always cold in their area, or did they have seasons?	It was pretty cold most of the time; it rarely reached 65 °F and was extremely cold in the winter.

History

K-W-L Chart

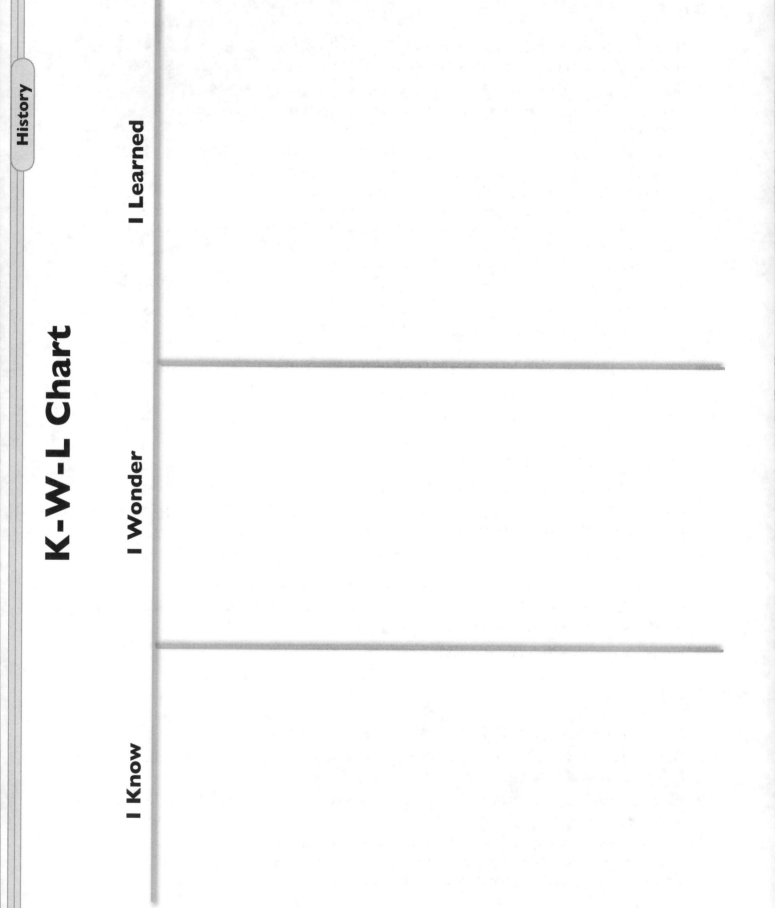

I Learned

I Wonder

I Know

Day 1

1. If possible, listen to a John Henry song to hear the tune to which his song is sung. The tune stays consistent, but the words differ depending on the source to which you refer.

2. Explain to your students that music, art, and legends reflect the mood of the public at a given point in time. Explain that legends are usually based on real people whose deeds are embellished or exaggerated.

3. Take a poll to see if more of your students know the legend of Johnny (Chapman) Appleseed or Davy Crockett. Discuss whichever legend the majority know. (*Johnny Appleseed (1774–1847) traveled throughout parts of Ohio, Indiana, and Illinois sowing apple seeds so that people would have fruit to eat. He was so generous that he never wore shoes, even in winter, as he gave away to others any shoes given to him. He demonstrated the pioneer spirit of conquering the wilderness by turning it into farmland. Davy Crockett (1786–1836) epitomized the frontiersman spirit. He represented Tennessee in the U.S. House of Representatives, fought in the Texas Revolution, and died at the Battle of the Alamo. He was so brave that it was said he killed a bear with his bare hands at the age of 3.*)

4. Make student copies of "John Henry: The First 'Man of Steel'" on page 22. Introduce any unfamiliar vocabulary:
   - ❖ **offended**—angered, displeased
   - ❖ **enshrined**—put in a place of honor; perfectly preserved
   - ❖ **feat**— extraordinary achievement
   - ❖ **riot**— a noisy, often violent public disorder caused by a group of protesters
   - ❖ **destruction**—wrecking; destroying
   - ❖ **machinery**—group of machines or a machine system

5. Distribute the copies and read aloud "John Henry: The First 'Man of Steel'" while your students follow along. If you discovered the tune, sing the song with your students twice.

6. Discuss the importance of the legend of John Henry to the workers of the early 20th century.

7. Make an overhead transparency and student copies of the organizer on page 24.

8. Discuss the meaning of the word *compare* (to examine two or more objects, ideas, people, etc., in order to note similarities and differences).

9. Fill in the graphic organizer as a class.

Day 2

1. Have your students get out their completed graphic organizers.

2. Display the overhead transparency, and write this question at its bottom: "Why did John Henry appeal to workers at the turn of the 20th century?"

3. Have your students independently write a short (3–5 sentence) response. Collect and evaluate these for understanding.

Extension: Find and copy whichever legend (Johnny Appleseed or Davy Crockett) you didn't discuss with your students as a group. Have your students read the legend and fill in the "Trait Comparison Chart" graphic organizers in groups of three.

History

John Henry: The First "Man of Steel"

In West Virginia in the early 1870s, men were making the Big Bend Tunnel on the Chesapeake and Ohio Railroad. Blasting was the best way to remove a lot of rock. To make the tunnel, they used long-handled hammers to pound a steel drill into the rock. This made the holes that they stuffed with blasting powder.

John Henry was a large African-American railroad worker whose strength amazed all those who met him. One day, a man brought a newly invented steam drill to the site. He wanted to sell it to the captain. He said that 20 workers swinging hammers couldn't make a hole as fast. John Henry was offended. He swore that he would beat that steam drill in a race. A song tells what happened next:

John Henry said to the captain, "Captain, you go to town;

Bring me back a twelve-pound hammer,

And I'll beat that steam drill down, O, Lord,

And I'll beat that steam drill down."

John Henry told his captain, "Now a man ain't nothing but a man.

But before I'll let that steam drill beat me down,

I'll die with this hammer in my hand, O, Lord,

I'll die with this hammer in my hand."

Now the man who invented that steam drill thought it was mighty fine;

But John Henry sunk the steel fourteen feet,

While the steam drill only made nine, O, Lord,

While the steam drill only made nine.

John Henry's captain came to him with $50 in his hand.

He laid his hand on his shoulder and said,

"This belongs to a steel-driving man, O, Lord,

This belongs to a steel-driving man."

John Henry said, "Captain, give the money to that li'l wife of mine."

Then he laid down his hammer and he died.

In heaven his hammer's enshrined, O, Lord,

In heaven his hammer's enshrined.

The real John Henry beat the steam drill, too. However, he died later, crushed under a large rock that fell from the tunnel's ceiling. The earliest known records about his feat appeared in 1900. Since then, songs and stories have kept John Henry's memory alive. He served as an important symbol at a time when workers feared being replaced by machines. Such fears led to worker riots and the destruction of machinery introduced into the workplace.

Traits Of *John Henry*	Shown By	Traits Of *workers at the turn of the 20th century*	Shown By
strong	ability to swing a 12-pound hammer	worried	wanted to keep their jobs
determined	wouldn't be outdone by a machine	determined	didn't want to be replaced by machines
hard-working	drove a steel drill deeper than a steam drill could	hard-working	eager to hold a job even if it was difficult or the hours long
admired	captain gave him $50, a huge sum at that time; considered a hero of the working man	afraid	rioting and destroying machinery

Why did John Henry appeal to workers at the turn of the 20th century?

At the turn of the 20th century, workers were afraid of losing their jobs to machines. Without jobs, they wouldn't have money for food or a roof over their heads. John Henry showed that a man could outdo a machine— and that's what workers hoped business owners would believe.

History

Traits Of _____	Shown By	Traits Of _____	Shown By

_____

_____

_____

_____

_____

1. Introduce the lesson by saying that you're taking a class vote to choose between two equivalent rewards (such as going out on the playground or free time in class or on computers). Then announce that only the boys can vote! Make a tally of the votes.

2. Next, ask your students how they felt when you announced that only the boys could vote on the class reward. How did the boys feel? Why? How did the girls feel? Why? Explain that at one time that was how all the decisions were made in the United States. There was a time when women could not vote.

3. Introduce unfamiliar vocabulary:

   ✧ **naturalized citizen**—a person from another nation who goes through a process to become a U.S. citizen (instead of being born in the U.S.)

   ✧ **servitude**—slavery

   ✧ **illegal**—against the law

   ✧ **suffragist**—a participant in the women's movement to win voting rights

   ✧ **inscription**—words carved or engraved on an object

   ✧ **amendment**—a formal change or addition to an existing document or record

4. Make student copies of "The Struggle for Women's Suffrage" on page 26. It is written at a 4.8 reading level, so you may want to read it as a class or pair weaker readers with stronger ones.

5. After the students finish reading the passage, ask your students these questions:

   • In what ways was Susan B. Anthony's trial illegal?

   • What was the significance of making the Justice Bell look just like the Liberty Bell?

   • How was a Constitutional amendment for women's suffrage better than state amendments for women's suffrage?

   • Why is the Nineteenth Amendment called the Susan B. Anthony Amendment?

6. Cut out a yellow transparent circle and a blue transparent circle the same size as the circles in the Venn diagram. (You can use red transparency if you don't have blue.) Make an overhead transparency and student copies of the Venn diagram on page 28.

7. Display the transparency and demonstrate how a Venn diagram works by placing a yellow transparent circle over one circle of the Venn diagram. Explain what this circle represents (*Susan B. Anthony*). Remove the yellow circle.

8. Next, place a blue transparent circle over the other circle. Explain what this circle represents (*Suffragists After 1906*).

9. Now put the yellow transparent circle back down. The intersection of the two circles will be green. Just as the color green is part yellow and part blue, the information in the intersection of the circles—details that apply to both Susan B. Anthony and suffragists after 1906—is a part of both categories.

10. Remove the transparent circles. As a class, have the students refer back to the passage to figure out what information goes in each part of the Venn diagram. The answers are shown in the completed Venn diagram on page 27. As much as possible, use the wording of your students.

History

The Struggle for Women's Suffrage

In 1872 Susan B. Anthony was arrested. Her crime? Voting! Anthony had read the Fourteenth Amendment to the U.S. Constitution. It stated, "All persons born or naturalized in the United States . . . are citizens." The Fifteenth Amendment stated, "The right of citizens of the United States to vote shall not be denied . . . on account of race, color, or previous servitude." Anthony knew that she should be allowed to vote—but at that time it was illegal for women to do so.

Susan B. Anthony

Anthony was a suffragist. She worked for the right of women to vote. She knew that she would be arrested for voting. But she didn't care. She wanted to bring the public's attention to the issue of women voting.

Anthony paid bail and left jail. Then she gave speeches about her cause at public meetings called rallies. At her trial, the judge would not even let Anthony speak! He said that women could not be witnesses. He ordered the jury to hand down a guilty verdict. Then he sent them home before they could even vote!

The judge fined Anthony $100 plus court costs. Anthony said that she would never pay it. She never did. But the judge did not put her in jail. If he did, she said that she would appeal to the U.S. Supreme Court. If she did that, the judge feared that she might win. So Anthony went free. She kept working for women to vote until she died in 1906. She had not achieved her goal. Still, just before her death, she said, "Failure is impossible."

Other women continued the fight. One woman paid for the casting of the Justice Bell in 1915. It looks just like the Liberty Bell, but it has a different inscription. Supporters gave the funds to pay for the Bell's tour costs. It toured the state of Pennsylvania from June until November. It went in a special truck made to carry it. It weighed one ton!

Parades, bands, and banners greeted the Justice Bell. Women stood on the truck next to it. They gave speeches. At each Pennsylvania rally, the women chanted, "Father, brother, husband, son, vote for Amendment Number One." It was up to male voters to pass the state's amendment to let women vote.

The amendment failed. But the women did not give up. They decided to get a Constitutional amendment. That would be even better than state amendments. It would give the right to vote to all American women. So the Justice Bell went to big rallies in Washington, D.C., and Chicago, Illinois. The cry for women's suffrage grew louder. At last Congress had to listen. On April 26, 1920, the Nineteenth Amendment to the U.S. Constitution went into effect. It gave all American women the right to vote. It is also known as the Susan B. Anthony Amendment.

Suffragists After 1906

- made the Justice Bell and took it on tour
- tried to get Pennsylvania state amendment passed, but failed
- saw the 19th Amendment to the U.S. Constitution pass
- voted legally

Both (overlap)

- worked for women's right to vote
- held rallies and gave speeches to promote women's suffrage

Susan B. Anthony

- voted illegally
- was arrested, tried, and found guilty for voting
- died before the 19th Amendment passed
- The 19th Amendment to the Constitution is named after her

History

Day I

1. Dim the lights in the room. Have your students close their eyes. Tell them that they are about to make a journey into the wilderness. They have no maps or cell phones. They will be gone for years. They will go down swift rivers. They will cross rugged mountains. They will meet friendly groups of people and unfriendly groups. Have them imagine the kinds of problems they might face.

2. Turn the lights on. Ask your students, "What should you pack, and why? How would you travel?" This discussion will help them to understand what the men faced on this journey.

3. Make student copies of "The Lewis and Clark Expedition" on page 30. Introduce vocabulary:

   ❖ **expedition**—a journey or voyage made for some specific purpose, such as exploration

   ❖ **weary**—exhausted, tired

   ❖ **vast**—huge

4. Read the article and discuss it as a class. It is written at a 4.9 reading level.

Day 2

1. Make overhead transparencies and student copies of both the "Events from the Lewis and Clark Expedition" on page 31 and the "Major Events Time Line" on page 33.

2. Introduce any unfamiliar vocabulary:

   ❖ **recruited**—signed up; enrolled

   ❖ **appendicitis**—inflammation of the appendix caused by a blockage or infection

   ❖ **confrontation**—a hostile disagreement that takes place face-to-face

   ❖ **interpreter**—a person who provides an oral translation between speakers who speak different languages

   ❖ **resumes**—continues; starts up again after an interruption

   ❖ **portage**—the act of carrying of boats, goods, etc., overland from one navigable water to another

   ❖ **grueling**—physically and/or mentally demanding to the point of exhaustion

3. Distribute student copies of "Events from the Lewis and Clark Expedition." As a class, read and discuss the events. Match events to places shown on the map.

4. Display the overhead transparency of the "Major Events Time Line." As a class, fill it in for the events of 1803.

5. Distribute the student copies of the "Major Events Time Line" graphic organizer. Divide the class into three groups. The students in the first group will fill in their graphic organizer for the events of 1804, the second group will do the events of 1805, and the third group will do the events for 1806.

6. Collect the graphic organizers and check for understanding.

7. Ask your students, "Which way was the best for showing the dates of major events: the article or the time line?" Guide them to understand that a lot of information can be gleaned quickly from a time line.

The Lewis and Clark Expedition

In 1803, President Thomas Jefferson bought the Louisiana Territory from France. This vast area of land lay between the Mississippi River and the Rocky Mountains. It went from the Gulf of Mexico to Canada. Jefferson hoped to find a water route that went from the Mississippi River to the Pacific Ocean. He hired Meriwether Lewis to explore and map the new land. Lewis asked William Clark to help him lead the expedition.

In December 1803, the pair hired 40 men and set up camp near St. Louis, Missouri. During the cold months the men built boats. They practiced shooting. The trip's leaders bought things to give to Native American chiefs. They purchased beads, pipes, belts, and knives.

On May 14, 1804, the group set out in three boats. Lewis and Clark thought that the round trip would take about 18 months. Instead it took more than two years. During that time the leaders kept logbooks. They drew pictures and made notes about plants and animals that they had never seen before.

Lewis and Clark

Traveling by boat was hard. Rocks lay below the water's surface, ready to damage a boat that sailed into them. Where the water was too low, the boats had to be pulled or carried by the men. Thousands of mosquitoes attacked them. Bears chased them. At last they reached the Great Plains. There, things improved for Lewis and Clark. They shot and ate buffalo.

But then the group met a Sioux tribe whose chief didn't like the gifts they gave him. He tried to take one of their boats. Luckily, they were able to end the situation peacefully. Lewis, Clark, and their weary group were glad to meet the friendly Mandan tribe. They spent the winter with them.

In April 1805, the group headed west again. They had three new members: a French trapper; his Native American wife, Sacagawea; and their baby boy. Sacagawea was quite helpful. She knew which plants they could eat and use for medicine. She saved most of their things when a boat flipped in swift flowing water. When the expedition needed horses in order to cross the Rocky Mountains, she got them from a tribe whose leader she knew.

Danger was constant. One man was blind in one eye and he had limited sight in the other. He accidentally shot Lewis! The group nearly starved crossing the Rocky Mountains. Yet just one man died on the trip.

The team got home on September 23, 1806. The men had covered 7,700 miles in one of the biggest adventures of all time.

Events from the Lewis & Clark Expedition

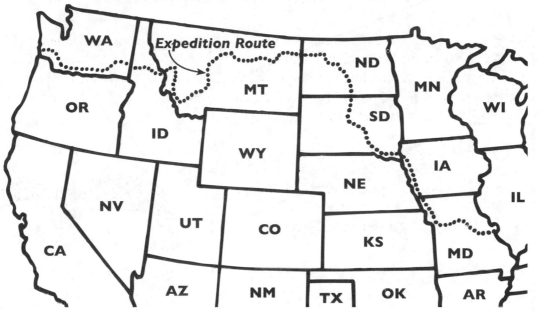

1803		
Jan. 18	Jefferson asks Congress for funds to explore the western part of North America.
Apr. 30	France sells the Louisiana Territory to the United States.
June 19	William Clark agrees to be Meriwether Lewis's co-leader for the expedition.
Oct. 15	Lewis and Clark meet in Indiana, where Clark had recruited men for the journey.
Dec. 13	The group sets up winter camp near St. Louis, Missouri.

1804		
May 14	The groups heads up the Missouri River.
Aug. 20	Sergeant Charles Floyd dies from appendicitis.
Sept. 25	Confrontation with Teton Sioux Indians ends peacefully.
Oct. 24	The group starts building Fort Mandan in North Dakota.
Nov. 4	Lewis and Clark hire a fur trader and his wife, Sacagawea, as interpreters.

1805		
Apr. 7	The team resumes their trip up the Missouri River.
June 13	They begin an 18-mile portage around the Great Falls of the Missouri River.
Sept. 11	The team begins 11 grueling days crossing the Rocky Mountains.
Nov. 18	Members of the team reach the coast of the Pacific Ocean.
Dec. 7	The expedition starts building Fort Clatsop in Oregon.

1806		
Mar. 23	The team begins its return trip.
July 3	The groups split in two—one looks for a shortcut home; the other explores more.
July 27	Two Blackfeet Indians try to steal from Lewis's group and are killed.
Aug. 12	The groups meet on the Missouri River near the mouth of the Yellowstone River.
Sep. 23	The expedition arrives back in St. Louis, Missouri.

From the Lewis and Clark Expedition, 1803

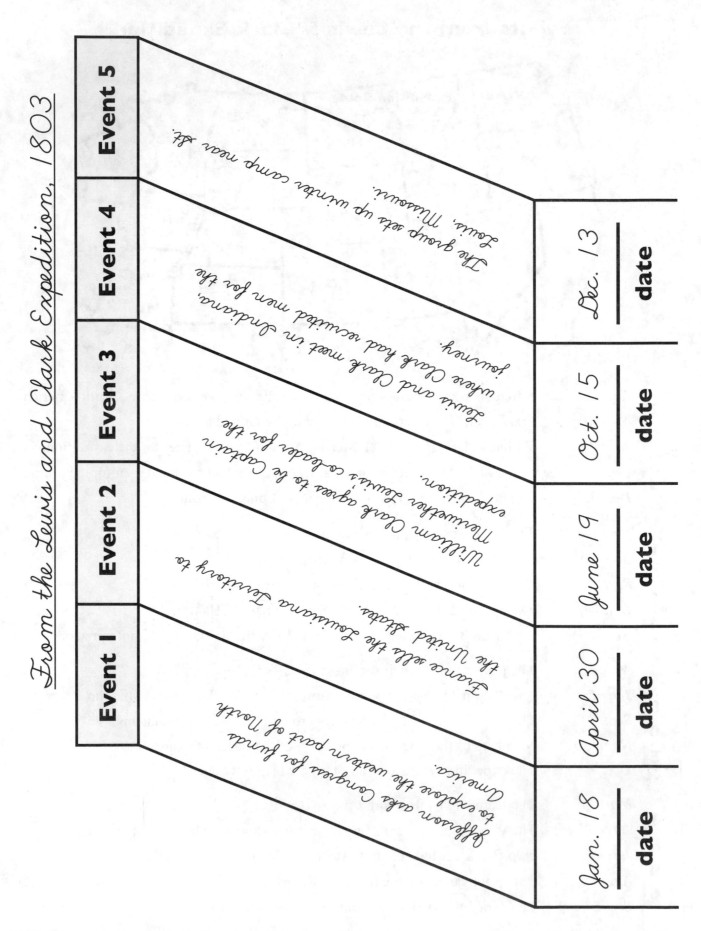

Event 1	Event 2	Event 3	Event 4	Event 5
Jefferson asks Congress for funds to explore the western part of North America.	France sells the Louisiana Territory to the United States.	William Clark agrees to be Captain Meriwether Lewis's co-leader for the expedition.	Lewis and Clark meet in Indiana, where Clark had recruited men for the journey.	The group sets up winter camp near St. Louis, Missouri.
Jan. 18 ___ date	April 30 ___ date	June 19 ___ date	Oct. 15 ___ date	Dec. 13 ___ date

History

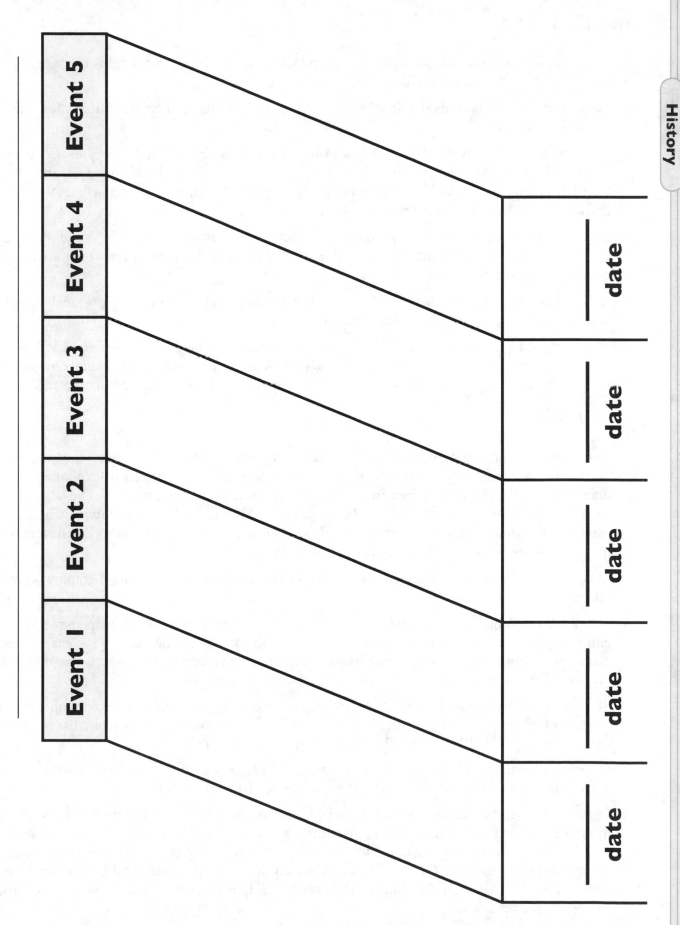

Geography

Day 1

1. This lesson is designed to follow the Lewis and Clark history lesson that begins on page 29. However, it can be done separately.

2. For student access, have available atlases, books, or maps of the United States that show the states' capital cities.

3. If you have not already done so, make an overhead transparency and student copies of "Events from the Lewis and Clark Expedition" on page 31. If you have not already done so, pre-teach the second group of unfamiliar vocabulary given on page 29. Then, read and discuss the events listed. Match them to the places shown on the map.

4. Remind your students that there were no states there when Lewis and Clark explored the land; it was all called the Louisiana Territory. The states were settled and cities built long after Lewis and Clark's adventure was over.

5. Ask your students to tell what was there when Lewis and Clark explored (the physical features, such as the rivers, waterfalls, mountains, and plains).

6. Have your students identify the 10 states that now boast a portion of the Lewis and Clark journey (*Missouri, Iowa, Nebraska, Kansas, North Dakota, South Dakota, Montana, Idaho, Oregon,* and *Washington*). Make a list of these states on the board or overhead. Keep this list posted.

Days 2–3

1. Explain to your students that every state in the United States has a capital. Ask your students to define what a capital city is. (It's not necessarily the largest city in a state.) A capital city is the place that has the physical offices and meeting places of the state government. The head of each state is a governor. He or she lives in the capital city. Most states have legislatures where the assemblymen and assemblywomen work. They meet in a building in the state capital to make major decisions about the state's budget, laws, and taxes.

2. Make an overhead transparency and student copies of the "United States Map" graphic organizer on page 36.

3. Distribute the copies and display the transparency. Ask your students if this map shows the entire United States (*no, it does not show Alaska or Hawaii*). Explain that this is a map of the continental United States—the 48 contiguous states plus the District of Columbia—and thus does not include the two newest states. *Contiguous* means "sharing a border."

4. Show your students how to use an atlas to find the state's capital (usually marked with a star) for Missouri (*Jefferson City*). Mark its location with a star on the transparency while the students do so at their seats. Tell them to use their neatest (and smallest) print.

5. Have your students use atlases, books, or maps to locate the capitals of the remaining nine states. They can also find this information on the Internet at *www.nationalatlas.gov*.

6. Have your students refer to their Lewis and Clark Expedition map to fill in the names of all the states it shows. They must use a globe, map, atlas, or textbook to find and fill in the rest of the states' names. They should make a compass rose at the bottom of the map and create an appropriate title (such as "Capital Cities of Selected States in the Continental U.S.A." or "Capital Cities of States That Were Part of the Lewis and Clark Expedition"). Collect the students' maps and check for accuracy.

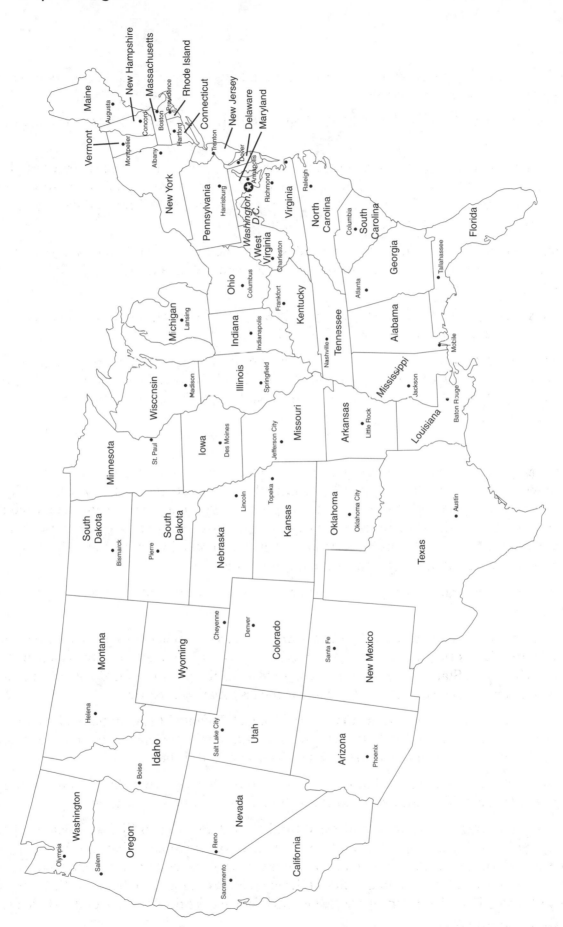

Geography

Geography

Day 1

1. Explain that a sunshine web has a central concept. Facts related to that concept are written on lines coming from the circle (like rays of light from the sun). You can show students a quick example by drawing a circle on the board or overhead transparency and writing a season inside it. Have students volunteer things related to that season and make sun "rays" with these ideas.

2. Make and distribute student copies of "Let's Get Recycling!" on page 38. Read the first paragraph aloud to the class. Stop and ask them to respond to the question it poses.

3. Read the second paragraph. Stop and ask your students if they have anything to add about landfills. If someone lives close to one or knows a person who drives a garbage truck, he or she may provide interesting insight.

4. Read the third paragraph. Stop and discuss the author's viewpoint on recycling. There are several clues in this paragraph indicating how the author feels about recycling. Ask your students to identify the clues.

5. Read the fourth paragraph. Stop and see if students have information to add about recycling.

6. Ask your class to read the fifth paragraph silently to themselves.

7. Make an overhead transparency and student copies of the "Sunshine Web" graphic organizer on page 40.

8. Display the transparency and distribute the student copies. Use two differently colored overhead pens and encourage your students to use two different color pencils. Write the word "Landfill" in one color inside the top circle and the word "Recycling" in a different color inside the bottom circle.

9. Have students refer to the article. What are the key points mentioned about landfills? They are given in the second and third paragraphs. Fill in the graphic organizer on the overhead while they do so at their seats. Be sure to explain to them how to figure out things (*since the article states that 35% of solid waste is recycled, that means that 65% of all solid waste goes into landfills*) and combine ideas (*trash is dumped in the big hole and covered with dirt*) to fit everything on the eight "rays."

Day 2

1. Have your students get out their "Let's Get Recycling!" article and "Sunshine Web" graphic organizers.

2. Put the students into teams of three. Each team is to reread the third, fourth, and fifth paragraphs of the article and choose the key points about recycling given. They are to write them on the lower portion of the graphic organizer.

3. Collect the graphic organizers and check for understanding.

Geography

Let's Get Recycling!

Look around the room. Most of what you see will one day be thrown out. Things wear out or break down. With computers, new models come out, so people throw out their old computers while they still work. Where will all these things go when they get tossed?

Today most waste goes to a landfill. A landfill is a big hole in the ground with a concrete or plastic liner to keeps chemicals from seeping into the groundwater around the landfill. Trash trucks filled with garbage drive to the landfill and dump their loads into the hole. Bulldozers cover everything with soil. In a landfill everything is thrown together in a heap. There are plenty of things that could be recycled. But once resources enter a landfill, they are stuck there. Landfills have other problems, as well. They must be located far away from people because they smell bad and attract rats. Also, we are running out of space to put all the trash.

Some places burn their trash in addition to using a landfill. But this isn't good, either, because it pollutes the air. Fortunately there's something you can do to help. You can recycle. Recycling lets things be used again. Most glass, paper, plastic, and metal is recyclable. When you recycle these things, it helps the environment. It saves space in landfills. And instead of wasting these resources, they get reused. Right now just 35 percent of all solid waste is recycled. That means that many of the things that could be recycled are not. In fact, paper takes up more space in landfills than any other thing. That's shocking, since paper is completely recyclable. And think of all the trees that could be saved if that paper had been reclaimed!

Some people must drive to a recycling center to drop off their recyclables. Others have their own recycle bins. They put their paper, metal, glass, and plastic into the bin and leave it at the curb. A special truck takes these things to a processing center where they are sorted. The paper is shredded and then mixed with water and wood pulp to make new paper. Glass, metal, and plastics are melted down. Then they are poured into molds to form new things. There's no limit to how many times something can get recycled.

Old cell phones and empty printer ink cartridges can be recycled, too. Parts from the cell phone are reused or melted down for the plastic and metal. The ink cartridges are refilled and sold again. Even old vehicles can be recycled. First, workers remove the tires and windows from an old vehicle. Then it enters a car crusher. Powerful jaws smash the car into a small, flattened rectangle that a crane loads onto a train car. The train carries it to a place where the steel is melted down and used to make new cars.

1	2	3	4	5	6	7
PETE	HDPE	PVC	LDPE	PP	PS	Other

Recycling Symbols
(the numbers stand for different types of plastic)

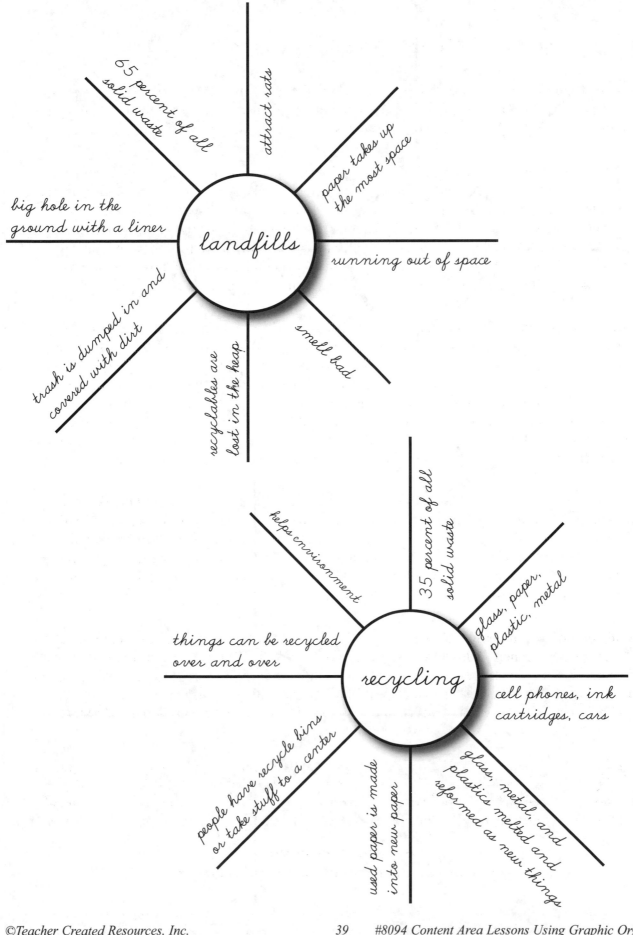

Geography

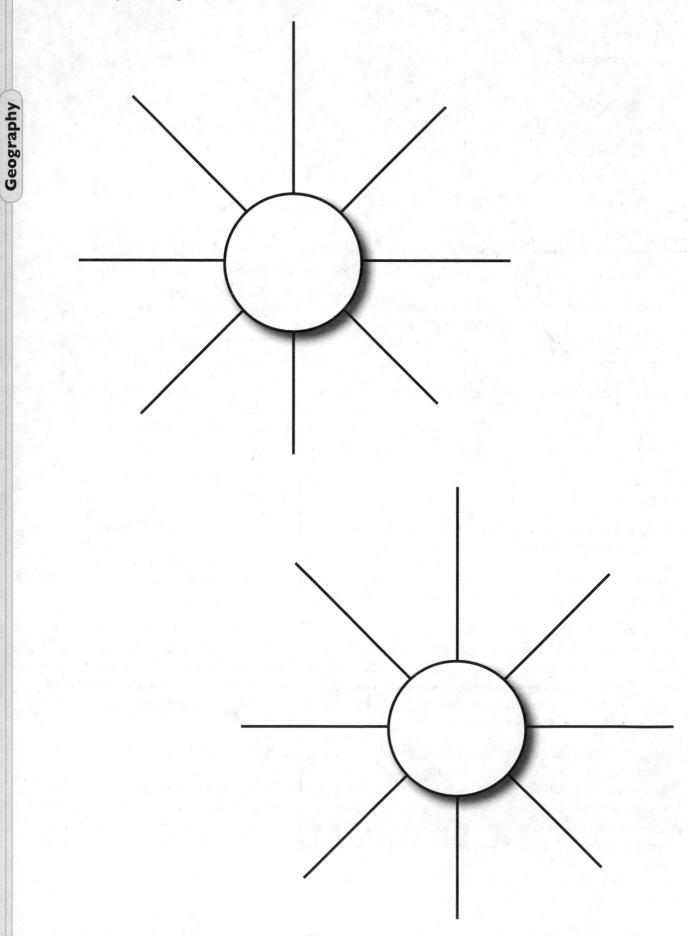

1. Introduce any unfamiliar vocabulary:

    ✧ **ecosystem**—the interaction of a community of organisms (plant and animal) with their physical environment

    ✧ **insecticides**—chemicals used to kill insects

    ✧ **species**—a group of organisms that resemble one another and can breed among themselves

    ✧ **prey**—an animal that is eaten by another animal

    ✧ **predator**—an animal that eats other animals

    ✧ **algae**—small green organisms that live in water. Algae were once thought to be plants but are now classified separately because they lack true roots, stems, leaves, etc.

    ✧ **drainage**—the process of carrying away excess water

2. Write this phrase on the board: "Changing Ecosystems: Think Twice Before Interfering." Tell your class that it is the title of an article you are going to read. Ask them to predict what they think the article will be about. If they're stumped, encourage them with questions such as, "Does the title make you think that the author thinks it's a good idea to change ecosystems?"

3. Make student copies of "Changing Ecosystems: Think Twice Before Interfering" on page 42. It is written at a 4.3 reading level. You may choose to pair students, let them read the article independently, or read it as a class. Be sure to point out on a map the places mentioned in the article: Arkansas; the Illinois River; Lake Michigan; Indonesia; and Malawi, Africa.

4. Make an overhead transparency and student copies of the "Bridge to Understanding" graphic organizer on page 44.

5. Display the transparency and distribute the student copies. You will fill in the transparency on the overhead while they follow along at their seats.

6. Discuss the analogy represented by the graphic organizer: the main part of a bridge is held up by its supports just as the main idea of a passage is supported by details.

7. As a class, decide on a main idea for the whole article. This is best done at the board because it requires the synthesis of ideas from multiple paragraphs. Have students give you what they think is the main idea. Combine their ideas together until you have the overall main idea: *People are often unhappy with the results when they cause great damage to ecosystems by getting rid of species, bringing in new species, or changing the environment.* Once you've established the main idea, record it on the transparency.

8. Ask your students to provide details from the article that support the main idea. Write these statements on the rest of the bridge. This requires the synthesis of ideas to form relevant sentences. If your students offer irrelevant details, such as "Wetlands provide homes for a wide variety of wildlife," do not write them on the bridge. Guide them to make a better choice through questioning, "Does that support the main idea? Remember, we are looking for examples of times when people were sorry after they changed ecosystems. Why did draining wetlands make people sorry?"

Geography

Changing Ecosystems:
Think Twice Before Interfering

People can cause big problems in ecosystems. Often they do not think what the long-term effects of an action will be. In the early 1980s the farmers in Indonesia used insecticides. They sprayed their crops. Why? They wanted to kill the bugs that ate the rice crop. But these chemicals also killed the spiders and bees that ate these bugs. To make matters even worse, the bad bugs got to the point where the chemicals could not kill them. There were more of them than ever before! So in 1986 the Indonesian government banned insecticides. Bees and spiders were brought in from another place and set free. At last the number of bad bugs fell. The rice harvest increased by 4.5 million tons a year.

Sometimes people get rid of a species on purpose. This is almost always a disaster. Why? It upsets food webs. Food webs need prey and predators to eat the prey. The people in Malawi, Africa, found this out the hard way. At first they wanted to get rid of all leopards. Leopards had killed their cattle and dogs. The government said the farmers could kill any leopard they saw. So they did. But then there were no leopards to eat the baboons. Soon there were way too many baboons. They ate the people's crops. They caused much worse problems than the leopards had!

People can damage the environment by bringing in a new species, too. More than 30 years ago, Asian carp were brought to farms in Arkansas. They were supposed to clean algae from ponds. But flooding swept them into the Illinois River. These fish taste bad. No one wants to eat them. Now they are eating too much of the food for fish that people do eat. People don't want them to get into the Great Lakes. They have put in underwater electrical gates to keep them from entering Lake Michigan.

People also cause trouble when they ruin environments. This has happened with wetlands. Many people think that wetlands are ugly. What they don't know is that they are essential. Wetlands provide homes for a wide variety of wildlife. They also provide good drainage for miles around. Yet people have filled in many of these damp, low-lying areas. Then they built farms, homes, and cities. But when wetlands are drained, mosquitoes breed out of control. At first scientists couldn't figure out why. Then they realized that rain water puddles offered the mosquitoes places to lay eggs. But the puddles could not provide homes for the ducks that eat them. To test their theory, scientists restored a 1,500-acre wetland. They found out that they were right. In a short time the number of mosquitoes fell by 90 percent!

Main Idea

People are often unhappy with the results when they damage ecosystems by getting rid of species, bringing in new species, or changing the environment.

Details

Farmers in Indonesia used chemicals to get rid of bad bugs but got rid of their predators, too—and ended up with more bad bugs than ever.

People in Africa killed so many leopards that baboons overran their crops.

U.S. farmers brought in Asian carp to clean up ponds, but the fish are taking all the food of tasty fish that people want to eat.

People filled in wetlands and ended up with too many mosquitoes and poor drainage.

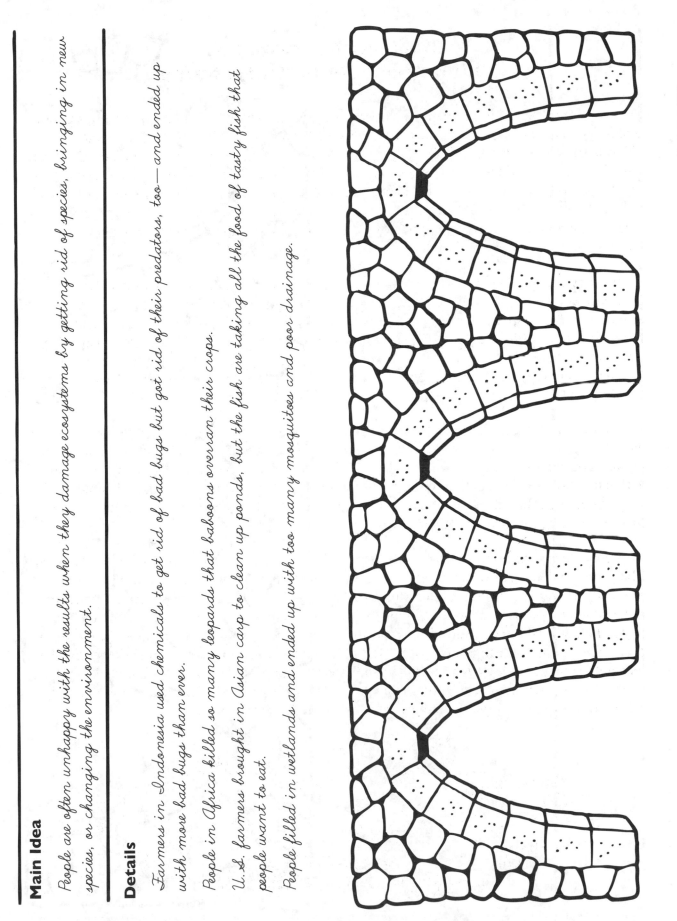

Geography

Main Idea

Details

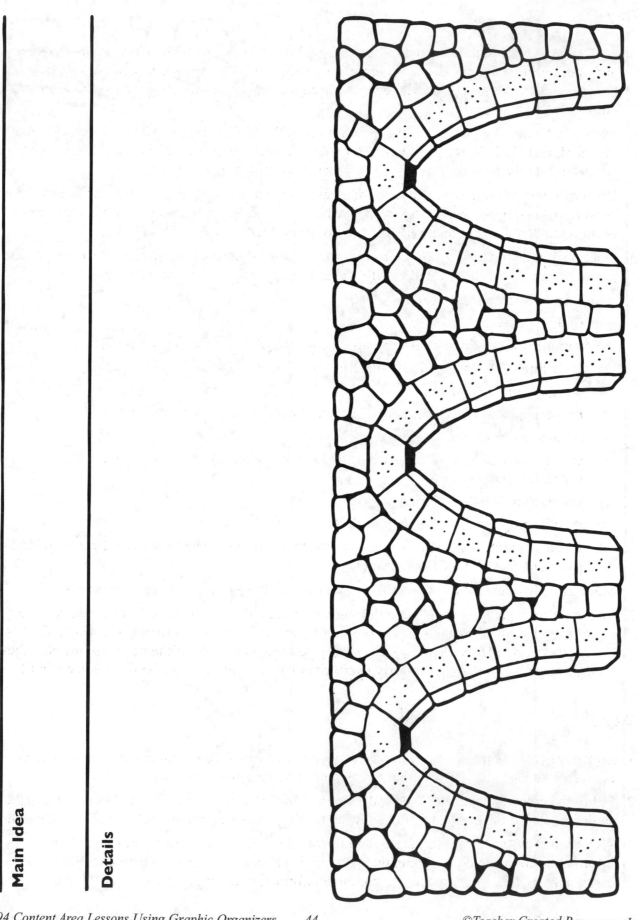

Day 1

1. Ask your students to define a natural hazard (*a danger caused by a naturally occurring event*) and name some (*hurricanes, earthquakes, tsunamis, tornadoes, floods, volcanoes, blizzards, droughts, etc.*). Make a list on the board. Discuss each one briefly to be sure your students know what each one is.

2. Display a United States map. Have them point out the U.S. Midwest, Atlantic Ocean, Eastern seaboard, and Gulf Coasts. Ask where they think each kind of hazard is most likely to occur and why. Discuss their choices, but do not correct any misconceptions yet.

3. Display a map of the world. Have the students point out the Atlantic, Pacific, and Indian Oceans, as well as Asia, India, and Australia. Ask where they think each kind of hazard is most apt to occur and why. Discuss their choices, but do not correct any misconceptions yet.

4. Tell your students that some of their ideas were right and others were wrong. Together you are going to read an article that will clarify where each kind of natural hazard occurs.

5. Introduce any unfamiliar vocabulary:

   ✧ **region**—area
   ✧ **tectonic plate**—huge pieces of Earth's crust that float on the liquid mantel
   ✧ **fault line**—the place on Earth directly above the edges of two tectonic plates
   ✧ **merge**—join together
   ✧ **Eastern seaboard**—the states and provinces that border the Atlantic Ocean
   ✧ **immense**—huge, massive
   ✧ **erodes**— the process by which Earth's surface is worn away by the action of water, ice, and wind
   ✧ **vegetation**—all the plants in an area
   ✧ **debris**—the remains of broken or destroyed things; ruins; rubble
   ✧ **Doppler radar**—a device that uses sound to determine speed (a police officer's handheld radar gun is a form of Doppler radar)

6. Make and distribute student copies of the article on page 46. Read it aloud to the class.

7. Stop after each paragraph and have the students point out on the U.S. and/or world maps the regions discussed. After the paragraph about floods, point out some major rivers in the U.S. and around the world (*Mississippi, Missouri, Nile, Yangtze, etc.*). Ask if the people living near these rivers worry about flooding. (Nearly every river has had catastrophic floods at some point.)

Day 2

1. Make an overhead transparency and student copies of the "Cause-and-Effect Matrix" graphic organizer on page 48. Display the transparency and distribute the student copies.

2. Fill in the column headings: "Natural Hazards" and "Places Most Likely to Occur." Have the students refer to the passage from yesterday to fill in the five natural hazards in the first column.

3. As a class, have students use the passage to complete the matrix. Note that some of the information in the completed graphic organizer is based on information combined from two paragraphs. Guide your students to combine information in this way, too.

Geography

Natural Hazards Can't Be Avoided

We cannot control Earth or its weather. That's why people around the world face natural hazards. Most are small. Their effects are minor. Others, like Hurricane Katrina, affect a region for years. When this storm hit the Gulf Coast in September 2005, it almost wiped out the cities of New Orleans, Louisiana, and Biloxi, Mississippi.

The kind of natural hazard you may face depends on where you live. People living near fault lines may have earthquakes. Earthquakes happen when Earth's tectonic plates shift. Even a minor one can cause a landslide. Major ones can make buildings, bridges, and roads cave in. Sewer, water, and gas lines may be ruined. Fires can start from broken gas lines, overturned gas stoves, and open flames (such as woodstoves and fireplaces). Earthquakes can happen wherever the edges of tectonic plates meet. The two most active fault lines in the United States are in California and Alaska.

Earthquakes also happen under the sea. This can cause tsunamis. A tsunami is a huge amount of water. It rushes across the sea. When it reaches a shore, this wall of water destroys all life, plants, and buildings. Nothing is left. Tsunamis are deadly disasters. The people on land have no warning. Tsunamis occur most often in the Pacific and Indian Oceans.

Storms cause natural disasters, too. Hurricanes form over the warm waters of the Atlantic Ocean in late summer and fall. A hurricane is actually a group of thunderstorms that merge to form a gigantic, swirling storm. Hurricanes strike the U.S. Eastern seaboard and Gulf Coast. Before the storm reaches a coast, the storm surge comes ashore. An immense amount of water rushes inland—sometimes for miles. This causes flooding and erodes the shore. Then the high winds hit. They wreck buildings, uproot trees, and destroy power lines. Hurricanes occur in the Indian and Pacific Oceans, too. In those places they are called typhoons (Asia), cyclones (India), or willy-willies (Australia).

Floods don't just occur as part of hurricanes; they can happen almost anywhere. A flood is often the result of snow melting or too much rain. Streams and rivers can't carry the water away fast enough, so they overflow their banks. Floods can wash away buildings, cars, and vegetation. Flash floods happen without warning. Heavy rain falls upstream. The people downstream may not even have rain. Suddenly a wall of water comes gushing down the stream. Bridges standing in the way of flash floods can be swept away. After any flood, the water recedes—and even the things that are still standing may be ruined. Homes may be filled with mud and debris.

Tornadoes can happen anywhere, too. But the states in the U.S. Midwest have more than any other place on Earth. These twisters often happen in spring or summer. A tornado forms inside a supercell. A supercell is a huge thundercloud. It forms a spinning funnel. When a twister touches down, it wrecks everything in its path. It will flatten buildings, uproot trees, and derail trains as if they were toys. People used to have little warning, but now Doppler radar can tell when one is forming. Then weather forecasters let people know that they must take cover.

Natural Hazard	Caused by	Effects	Places Most Likely to Occur
earthquake	sudden shifting of Earth's tectonic plates	cracks ripped open in ground; landslides, buildings, bridges, and streets cave in	along tectonic plate lines; most active fault lines in U.S. are in California and Alaska
tsunami	undersea earthquake or volcanic eruption	complete destruction of all life, buildings, and vegetation where tsunami comes ashore	Pacific and Indian Oceans
hurricane/ typhoon	thunderstorms that join together over warm water and start to swirl	storm surge can cause massive flooding and erosion; high winds can collapse buildings, destroy power lines, and uproot trees	along the U.S. Eastern seaboard and Gulf Coast; along the Indian, Asian, and Australian coasts
flood	too much rain; hurricane storm surge; rapid melting of snow in the spring	washes away buildings, cars, vegetation; when water recedes, even things that are still standing may be ruined by tons of mud	along shorelines and rivers
tornado	rotation in a supercell (huge cloud that's part of a thunderstorm)	destroys almost everything in its path—flattens buildings, uproots trees, and derails trains	in the U.S. Midwest

Geography

	Caused by	**Effects**	

Day 1

1. This lesson should be part of the unit about the processes that change the face of Earth (volcanoes, erosion, earthquakes, landslides, drought, etc.). The first part can be done at the beginning of the unit; however, the other days must be done after you have studied erosion and earthquakes.

2. Make and distribute student copies of "Volcanoes Change the Earth's Surface" on page 50.

3. Have the students read the passage. It is written at a 4.7 reading level.

4. Make an overhead transparency and student copies of the "Acrostics Summary Grid" graphic organizer on page 52. Display the transparency and distribute the student copies.

5. Fill in the chart with the class. Let the students suggest words and phrases for each letter. This is a great time for you to clear up any misconceptions that may arise.

6. An answer key is provided on page 51, but these are not the only possible answers.

Day 2 *(after learning about erosion)*

1. Wipe clean the overhead transparency. Write "Erosion" on it and make student copies of it.

2. Display the overhead transparency and distribute the student copies.

3. Fill in the organizer as a class. Accept student suggestions. Here are possible answers:

   E Erosive processes include the action of flowing water, glaciers, wind, and waves.
   R Rill, or gully, erosion occurs when water runs downhill fast (such as after a heavy rain).
   O Ocean waves erode (wear away) the shore.
   S Streams and rivers move more tons of rock and dirt than any other process.
   I Increasing the amount of flowing water causes an increase in erosion.
   O Over millions of years, flowing water and wind erosion carved out the Grand Canyon.
   N No-till is a farming method to cut erosion by leaving the prior crop in place to hold soil.

Day 3 *(after learning about earthquakes)*

1. Wipe clean the overhead transparency. Write "Earthquake" on it. Put the "qu" on one line. Then make student copies of the graphic organizer.

2. Display the overhead transparency and distribute the student copies.

3. Fill in the organizer as a class. Accept student suggestions. Here are possible answers:

   E Earth's crust is made of huge tectonic plates.
   A Alaskan earthquake of 1964 was worst ever recorded in North America.
   R Richter scale is used to measure the strength/intensity of earthquakes.
   T Tectonic plates grinding against each other cause earthquakes.
   H Hypocenter, or focus, of a quake is the spot in Earth's mantle where the rocks first break.
   QU Quakes under the sea can trigger tsunamis (such as the one in December 2004.)
   A Aftershocks may occur after a large quake and can continue for up to a year.
   K Knocking down buildings and bridges are some of the worst hazards of quakes.
   E Epicenter is the point on Earth's surface right above the focus and has the worst shaking.

Note: The "Acrostics Summary Grid" graphic organizer can be used in any content area. It can be used with any word that has nine letters (or fewer).

Volcanoes Change the Earth's Surface

Earth's crust is like a giant cracked eggshell. The huge pieces of this shell are called tectonic plates. Volcanoes happen along the cracks between these plates. The most violent eruptions occur after pressure builds up inside a volcano. When a volcano erupts, magma (melted rock) from deep within Earth spills out. When it flows onto Earth's surface, it is called lava.

Lava flows toward the lowest point. It usually only goes about three feet (1 m) an hour, but it may move up to 25 miles per hour (40 kph). Eventually it cools and hardens into one of three kinds of igneous rock. They are basalt, pumice, or obsidian. Basalt is a dark, heavy rock that has lots of iron in it. It makes up most of Earth's ocean crust. Pumice is light-colored and full of air holes. It is a kind of glass that's so light it can float! Obsidian is a shiny, dark glass-like rock that forms when lava cools fast.

A volcano doesn't just spew lava. It also releases ash and noxious gases. The gases are carbon dioxide, carbon monoxide, and ammonia. If these toxic gases stay low to the ground, living things will die. If the gases go into the atmosphere, they make acid rain. This causes plants to die hundreds of miles away. Steam and other gases may constantly come from small vents in an active volcano. Scientists call a volcano active as long as it releases gases.

A volcano often looks like a giant cone. Inside the cone are conduits. They are like tubes that connect to magma chambers. Magma moves up the conduits during an eruption. As it rises, gases and ashes separate from it. They form hot clouds. These clouds rise miles into the sky and glow at night. The ash can stay in the atmosphere for up to a year. It can block sunlight and change weather conditions around the world.

Did you know that most of Earth's volcanoes lie under the sea? Undersea volcanoes erupt daily. After years of eruptions, lava builds up. In some places this has caused the volcanoes to show above the water's surface. Iceland and all of Hawaii formed this way. Since lava is still flowing, each day new land is formed in Hawaii.

There are about 500 active land volcanoes. Most of them do not erupt often. When they do, big chunks of solid rock called volcanic bombs may get thrown into the air. If a volcano erupts with great force, it can cause a landslide. Rocks and soil from the volcano's sides fall downhill. Such slides flow like raging rivers. They wreck everything in their path.

There are more than six billion people on Earth. Many live in the shadow of an active volcano. No one can tell for sure when a volcano will erupt, but scientists are looking for better ways to tell when one will happen. They want to give people warning so they can escape.

50

V	Violent eruptions occur when the pressure inside a volcano becomes too great.
O	Obsidian is a shiny, dark, glass-like rock that forms when lava cools quickly.
L	Lava flows can move at 25 mph. Lava is the name for melted rock on Earth's surface (below the surface, it's called magma).
C	Conduits are like tubes that connect Earth's surface to magma chambers. Magma travels up these conduits during an eruption.
A	Ash is often thrown into the air during volcanic eruptions. The ash can stay in the atmosphere and change weather conditions around the world.
N	Noxious (toxic) gases are often part of an eruption. If these gases stay low to the ground, many living things die from them long before the lava reaches them.
O	The ocean floor has volcanoes erupting almost all the time. Over time, the lava builds up until it reaches past the water's surface. All of Hawaii was formed this way.
E	Eruptions can cause parts of a volcano to start sliding down the mountain in a massive rock and landslide.
S	Steam and gas may be constantly released from small vents in an active volcano.

Science

Day 1

1. Bring in some magnets. Show the students how they work by having them attract and repel each other. Explain that you are going to study the force called magnetism.

2. Ask your students to share with you what they already know about magnets.

3. Make student copies of "May the Force Be With You" on page 54. Introduce any unfamiliar vocabulary:
   - ❖ **attract**—draw closer
   - ❖ **repel**—push away
   - ❖ **refrigerator**—your students know what this is; just be sure they recognize the word
   - ❖ **repeatedly**—over and over again
   - ❖ **restore**—put back the way it was
   - ❖ **levitation**—floating in the air without support

4. Have your students read the passage. It is written at a 4.8 reading level, so you may want to read it as a whole class or pair stronger readers with weaker ones.

5. Questions for discussion:
   - Name some things that you know for sure are not magnetic. (*paper, wood, glass, gold, plastic, etc.*)
   - Tin is not a magnetic metal. So why is a tin can magnetic? (*because it's actually an iron can coated with tin*)
   - What would be a bad thing to put near a compass? (*a strong magnet or piece of iron*) Why? (*The compass needle could respond to the close magnetic field rather than Earth's magnetic field.*)

6. Make an overhead transparency and student copies of the "Magnet Summaries" graphic organizer on page 56.

7. Introduce the graphic organizer with this analogy: Just as magnets are drawn to steel, magnet words draw facts to themselves. Display the transparency and distribute the student copies of the graphic organizer. Write "What's a magnet?" "magnetic force" and "atoms" between the prongs of the magnets. These are the main ideas (or "magnet words") for the paragraphs. On the horseshoe magnet, the students are to write the relevant facts or terms from the passage. Then they must use those terms to write a summary on the piece of steel.

8. Go through the passage and determine the words that should go on each horseshoe magnet for the first five paragraphs.

9. As a class, compose the summary for the three bars of steel. Answers are given on page 55 for your guidance, but use the students' words as much as possible.

Day 2

1. Distribute fresh copies of the "Magnet Summaries" graphic organizer. Pair the students. Have your students write "Magnetic Earth" between the horseshoe magnet prongs of the first magnet and "Uses for Magnets" between the prongs of the second magnet.

2. Have the pairs find the terms from the final two paragraphs of the passage and write these words on the horseshoe magnets. Then they compose summaries for the two bars of steel. Tell the students that the third section of the graphic organizer is not used this time.

3. Collect their graphic organizers to check for understanding.

May the Force Be With You

A magnet is a piece of metal or stone with the power to attract or repel certain other materials. This magnetic force is invisible. But we can see its results when one magnet is drawn toward or pushed away from another.

There are different kinds of magnetic materials. Magnets occur naturally in lodestone. This rock is made of iron ore. We mine the iron ore. Then we add other substances to it. This changes it into the stronger metal we call steel. Steel is less magnetic than iron. Yet even steel with very little iron in it is still magnetic.

Around any magnet lies a magnetic field. This is the area around a magnet that affects other magnetic materials. Some parts of a magnet—usually the ends—have more magnetic force. Distance is also an important factor in magnetic force. The closer the item, the stronger its magnetic force. If you put two magnets on opposite sides of a piece of paper, they will still attract. But if you put two magnets on different sides of a thick piece of wood, the distance is too great.

Magnetic force can move through things such as paint. That's why magnets stick to your refrigerator. The fridge is made of painted steel. A "tin" can is iron coated with tin. So tin cans are magnetic.

All the atoms face the same way in a magnet. That's why a magnet has a "north" end and a "south" end. The north end of one bar magnet attracts the south end of another. And the north end of one magnet repels the north end of another. If a magnet gets heated or repeatedly dropped, its atoms will jumble. It will no longer be a magnet. But rubbing it against a powerful magnet can restore it.

Our Earth is magnetic. How do we know that? If a magnet is hung in the air and can move freely, it will point toward Earth's magnetic north pole. This is the basis for a compass. Since a compass needle always points north, people can get an idea of where they are. Compasses are built right into the control panels on ships and planes. During a bad storm in the sky or sea, they help pilots and captains stay on course.

People use magnets for other things, too. Magnets can sort steel from other scrap metals. They can find iron pipes behind brick walls. A magnetic resonance imaging (MRI) machine uses powerful magnets to make a computer picture of the brain. This does not hurt the patient and can help doctors find out what is wrong. Magnetic levitation trains move due to strong magnetic fields. One field is on the rail. The other is on the bottom of the train itself. These two fields repel each other. This causes the train to float a few inches above the track. These trains can go very fast.

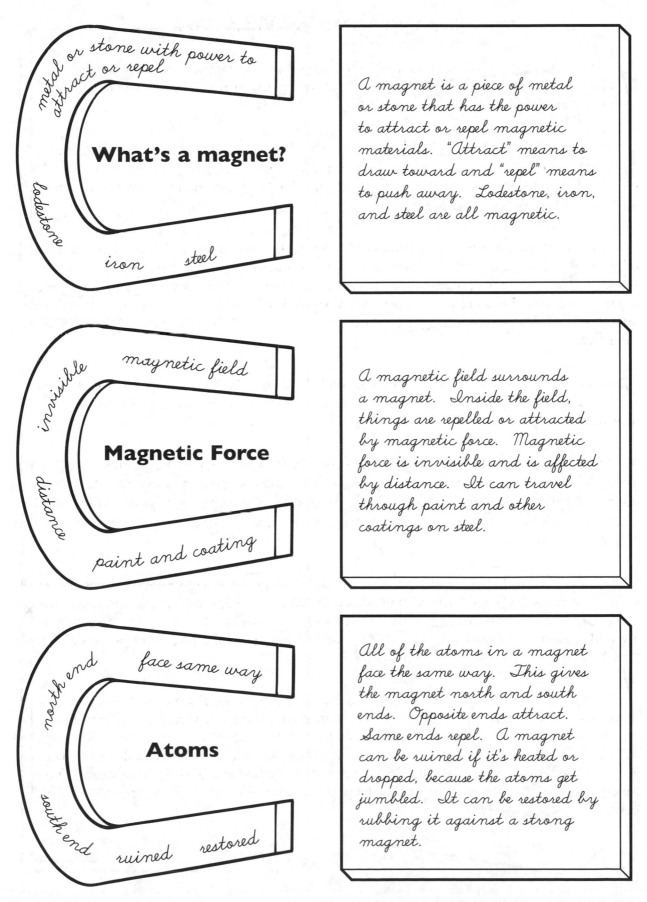

What's a magnet?

metal or stone with power to attract or repel

lodestone

iron　　steel

A magnet is a piece of metal or stone that has the power to attract or repel magnetic materials. "Attract" means to draw toward and "repel" means to push away. Lodestone, iron, and steel are all magnetic.

Magnetic Force

invisible　magnetic field

distance

paint and coating

A magnetic field surrounds a magnet. Inside the field, things are repelled or attracted by magnetic force. Magnetic force is invisible and is affected by distance. It can travel through paint and other coatings on steel.

Atoms

north end　face same way

south end　ruined　restored

All of the atoms in a magnet face the same way. This gives the magnet north and south ends. Opposite ends attract. Same ends repel. A magnet can be ruined if it's heated or dropped, because the atoms get jumbled. It can be restored by rubbing it against a strong magnet.

Science

Day 1

1. Make an overhead transparency and student copies of "Cold-Blooded Vertebrates" on page 58.

2. Display the overhead transparency without distributing the copies. Keeping most of the passage covered, ask your students to turn the side headings into questions. They will then read to find the answers.

3. Make a T-chart on the board while the students do so on paper. Here are the questions from the side headings for the first column:

What is a cold-blooded animal?	*What traits do all vertebrates have?*
What makes an animal a vertebrate?	*What were the early vertebrates like?*

4. Introduce any unfamiliar vocabulary:

   ✧ **complex**—very complicated, not simple, involved

   ✧ **symmetrical**—can be divided into at least two identical parts

   ✧ **invertebrate**—an animal that does not have a spine (vertebrae)

   ✧ **evolved**—changed slowly (often over a long period of time)

   ✧ **internal**—inside

5. Distribute copies of the article and read it as a class. Do not stop to answer the questions the first time through.

6. Reread the article. This time have the students raise their hands when you read something that answers one of the questions. Have them identify the answer in the text. Underline it on the transparency. Have the students copy the answers onto their T-charts.

Day 2

1. Make an overhead transparency and student copies of the graphic organizer on page 60.

2. Display the transparency and distribute the copies. Fill in the chart together, using this script to elicit student responses (the answers are provided on the completed graphic organizer on page 59):

   • What's the main topic that goes at the top?

   • The topic's definition goes in the next rectangle. What should we write there?

   • What are the three kinds of cold-blooded vertebrates?

   • What is the skin covering of each one like?

   • Give three examples of each kind. Name one of each of the three different kinds of fish explained in the article. What are the traits of *all* vertebrates?

   • What are the traits of only some vertebrates? (Remind them that in this case, "some" actually means "most.")

3. Collect the graphic organizers and check for understanding. Prior to a test or quiz on this material, return each student's graphic organizer and explain how to use it to study.

Cold-Blooded Vertebrates

You are warm-blooded. This means that your body controls its temperature. But only mammals and birds have warm blood. Ninety-seven percent of the animals on Earth have cold blood.

Cold-Blooded Animals

Cold-blooded animals have little control over their body temperature. If their environment is warm, so are they. If their surroundings are cold, they are, too. This is why you may have seen a snake or turtle lying in the sun. It's how they get warm. It's also why no cold-blooded animals live in the Arctic Circle or Antarctica. Those places are too cold for them.

Vertebrates

A vertebrate (VUR-tuh-briht) is an animal with a skull and vertebrae (VUR-tuh-bray). That's the scientific word for the bones that form a spine. Cold-blooded vertebrates include fish, reptiles, and amphibians. Before they hatch or are born, all vertebrates have cartilage skeletons. Cartilage is the tough yet flexible tissue that gives shape to your nose and ears. A few vertebrates, such as sharks and rays, have a cartilage skeleton all their lives. They never have solid bones. But in most vertebrates, bone replaces the cartilage. This happens slowly as the animal grows.

Vertebrate Traits

Each vertebrate has a skull. It protects a complex brain. The brain controls a complicated nervous system. In fact, all vertebrates have nervous systems similar to ours. Our nervous system lets us use our senses. Vertebrates can see, hear, feel, taste, and smell. The ears, eyes, and nose are on the animal's head.

All vertebrates are symmetrical. The left and right sides of their bodies are just alike. Fish have gills, but many vertebrates breathe with lungs. A rib cage protects the lungs. The number of ribs differs by species. In general, vertebrates are larger and faster moving than invertebrates.

Early Vertebrates

The first vertebrates appeared about 500 million years ago. They were small and lived in water. They had bony plates covering their heads and bodies. They did not have jaws. They ate bits of dead animals or small animals on the sea floor.

Then vertebrates evolved. About 440 million years ago, they developed skeletons. These skeletons had bones covered by muscles and flesh (and scales in reptiles and fish). A skeleton was an internal frame. Muscles could attach to it. Next, they developed jaws and teeth. This let them catch and eat bigger food. A few jawless fish are still around. The most common is the eel.

Science

Cold-Blooded Vertebrates

| an animal with a skull . . . |

```
        fish              reptiles          amphibian
      (scales)            (scales)         (soft, moist
                                               skin)
```

shark   trout   eel   lizard   snake   turtle   frog   toad   salamander

Traits of All	**Traits of Some**
• start out with cartilage skeletons	• develop skeletons of bone
• skull and spine	• jaws
• complex brain and nervous system with senses	• lungs protected by a rib cage
• symmetrical	
• larger and faster than most invertebrates	

Science

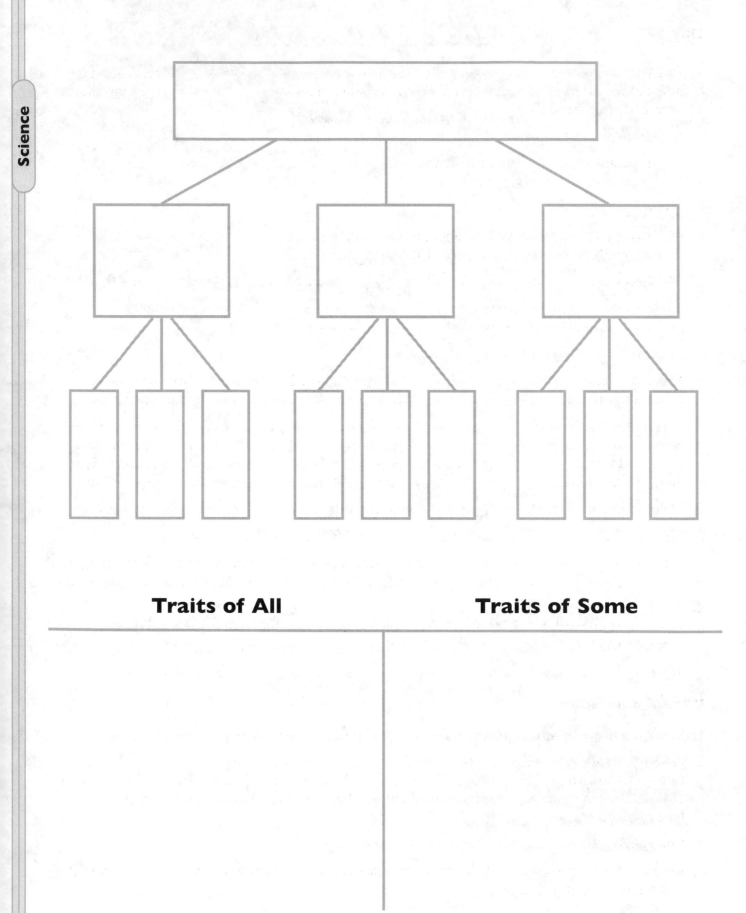

Traits of All   **Traits of Some**

Day 1

1. Ask your students to volunteer whatever information they know about bees. Make a list on the board of the information they provide. Put a question mark after any "facts" that you know are wrong or are questionable.

2. Introduce any unfamiliar vocabulary:

   ✧ **metamorphosis**— a marked series of developmental changes in the form or structure of an animal; transformation

   ✧ **eventually**—after a time; at last

   ✧ **royal jelly**—a milky yellow, high-protein syrup secreted by worker bees as food for all young larvae and as the only food for the queen bee

   ✧ **beebread**—a mixture of pollen and honey fed by bees to their non-queen larvae

   ✧ **cocoon**—a silky envelope spun by the larvae of many insects to serve as a covering while they are in the pupa stage

   ✧ **emerges**—comes out

3. Make an overhead transparency and student copies of "The Life Cycle of a Bee" on page 62. It is written at a 3.4 reading level, so your students should be able to read it independently.

4. Display the transparency. Ask your students to identify how the different kinds of bees look at each of the four stages. For example, the eggs look identical. But the ends of the queen larva curl in a different direction than the others. The worker larva is smallest. Jot notes about these things on the transparency and have the students make the same notes on their copies.

5. Make an overhead transparency of the completed "Life Cycle" graphic organizer on page 63.

6. Make student copies of the blank "Life Cycle" graphic organizer on page 64.

7. Display the transparency and distribute the student copies. Make sure the students have "The Life Cycle of a Bee" passage to refer to. Have the students cut out the pictures for the queen bee and glue them in order on the organizer.

8. Ask your students to add relevant details (such as the fact that an egg hatches into a larva on day 4) from "The Life Cycle of a Bee" article to their graphic organizers.

Day 2

1. Make and distribute fresh student copies of the blank "Life Cycle" graphic organizer.

2. Assign half of your students the task of filling it in for drones and the other half the task of filling it in for worker bees. Using "The Life Cycle of a Bee" article and their completed graphic organizers from yesterday, students should cut out the correct drawings and write labels for their type of bee.

3. Collect the graphic organizers and check for understanding.

4. Retain these graphic organizers so that your students may use them in the language arts expository writing lesson that begins on page 65.

Science

The Life Cycle of a Bee

Most insects go through metamorphosis. This means that they go through a major change in stages. Butterflies, moths, ants, beetles, mosquitoes, and bees all have a life cycle that includes metamorphosis.

Bees start out as eggs, hatch as larva, develop into a pupa, and eventually become an adult. The amount of time it takes each bee to go through these stages depends upon the kind of bee it is. Males, called drones, take 24 days to go through the four stages. Females, called workers, take 21 days. The queen bee takes just 16 days, even though she grows the largest.

First, the queen lays a tiny, white, oval egg at the base of a cell in the honeycomb. After three days, a larva hatches. It looks like a tiny worm. The worker bees feed the larva royal jelly for three days and beebread for six days. The queen larva is fed only royal jelly. Each larva grows bigger rapidly. On the tenth day, the larva spins a cocoon around itself within the cell.

Inside the cocoon, a pupa develops. It begins to look like an insect instead of a worm. The pupa grows eyes, two pairs of wings, and three pairs of legs. At last it emerges as an adult bee. The queen bee is the biggest. The worker bees are the smallest. Drones are between the size of worker bees and queen bees.

	EGG	LARVA	PUPA	ADULT BEE
QUEEN	Days 1–3	Days 4–9	Days 10–15	Day 16
WORKER	Days 1–3	Days 4–9	Days 10–20	Day 21
DRONE	Days 1–3	Days 4–9	Days 10–23	Day 24

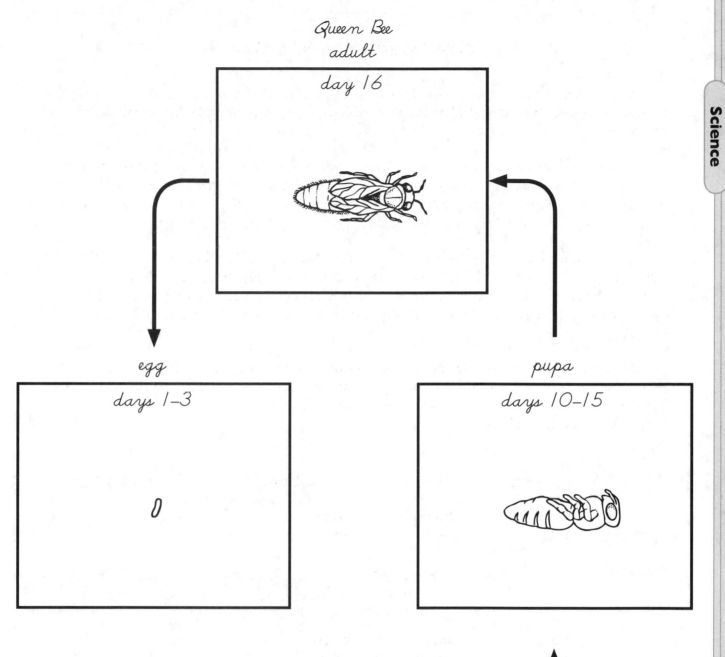

Queen Bee
adult

day 16

egg

days 1–3

𝒪

pupa

days 10–15

larva

days 4–9

Science

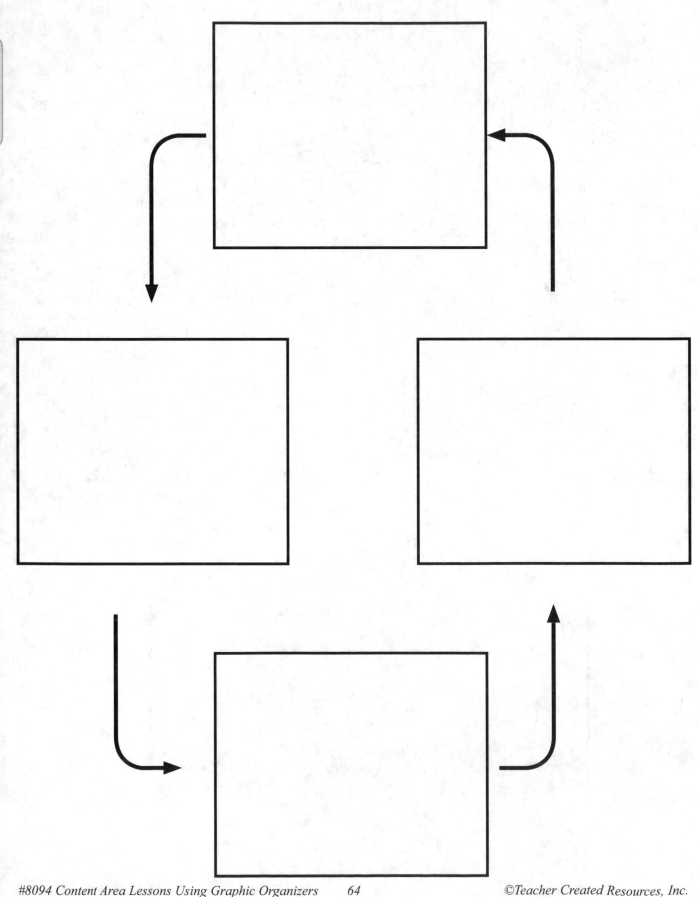

Day 1

1. This lesson is meant to follow the life-science lesson "Bees" that begins on page 61. However, if you want to do it separately, distribute to your students copies of "The Life Cycle of a Bee" on page 62. Have them read the information. It is written at a 3.4 reading level.

2. To introduce this lesson, write and display this poem on an overhead transparency. Read it aloud.

> ## The Bee
> ### by Isaac Watts
>
> | | |
> |---|---|
> | How does the little busy bee | How skillfully she builds her cell! |
> | Improve each shining hour, | How neatly she spreads the wax! |
> | And gather nectar all the day | And labors hard to store it well |
> | From every opening flower! | With the sweet honey she makes. |

3. Have your students define nectar (*sweet liquid produced by flowers*), honey (*a thick, sweet fluid made from nectar by bees and stored as food*) and beeswax (*a solid, yellowish substance secreted by bees*). Use this opportunity to clear up any misconceptions they may have.

4. Introduce any unfamiliar vocabulary:
   - **pollen**—fine, powdery, yellowish grains produced by flowers as part of reproduction
   - **beebread**—a mixture of pollen and honey fed by bees to their non-queen larvae
   - **royal jelly**—a milky, yellow, high-protein syrup secreted by worker bees as food for all young larvae and as the only food for the queen bee larvae

5. Make student copies of "Being a Bee" on page 67. Decide if you want students to read it as a whole group, independently, or in pairs. It is written at a 4.5 reading level.

6. After everyone finishes reading the passage, redisplay the poem. Questions for discussion:
   - Which kind of bee is referred to in Watts's poem? (*female, or worker bees*)
   - How do you know? (*They're the ones who get nectar, build cells, spread wax, and make honey.*)

Day 2

1. For the poster project, decide in advance if you want your students to select their own type of bee or if you want to assign one. The easiest bee to write about is the drone, then the queen, with the worker being the most difficult.

2. Make and distribute student copies of the "Poster Planner" graphic organizer on page 68. Explain that the students are to take information from two passages, "The Life Cycle of a Bee" and "Being a Bee," to create a unique poster about a drone, worker, or queen bee (whichever you assigned to them or they chose). The poster must be attractive, colorful, and educate the viewer. The students can choose to do the poster in portrait or landscape mode; the graphic organizer will work for either display.

3. Have each student use a highlighter to identify in both pieces the facts that they want to include on the poster. Check their highlighted passages to be sure they're on the right track.

Writing

Day 2 *(cont.)*

4. If your students did the life-science lesson on bees, they can use their "Life Cycle" graphic organizers if it is for the type of bee for which they are making the poster. It would make an ideal central image. Otherwise, you can make copies of the "Life Cycle" graphic organizer from page 64 for students who choose to include that diagram on their posters.

5. Keep this list of steps posted where your students can refer to it:

   ☞ Decide what pictures and facts to include.

   ☞ Use the graphic organizer to prepare the layout. (Use pencil so you can move things around if you want.)

   ☞ Have the teacher check your graphic organizer before you begin on the poster board. Once it's been checked, do not change it.

   ☞ On the poster, do all drawings in pencil. Color with markers or crayons.

   ☞ Make light pencil lines with a ruler so that you will have straight lines on which to write.

   ☞ Write all information in pencil. Go over all information with a black felt-tip marker.

   ☞ Erase all stray marks and the lines on which you wrote.

   ☞ Make sure to put your name on the poster.

6. If you have an example of a completed poster, share it with the class.

Days 3–5

1. Students prepare their posters. Be sure to circulate to help them with any problems that occur.

2. The posters should be graded on the back and then displayed in the hall for other classes to enjoy. This would be an ideal project to have on display for open house.

Note: After the first time you do this lesson, ask two of your students if you may keep their completed posters to show as an example for the next time you teach it.

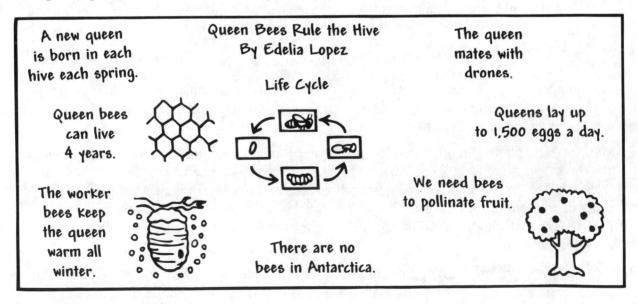

Being a Bee

You have probably heard the saying "busy as a bee." People say it because bees are always busy. They are active year round.

For more than 10,000 years people have relied on bees. People used beeswax for candles and honey for food. Bees play an important role in pollinating the plants that give us fruits and vegetables. Without them, our crops would be cut by one-third. That means that instead of 30 ears of corn growing, there would be just 20. Bees do this essential work on every continent except Antarctica. There are no flowers there.

In January, the bees eat the honey stored in their hive. During the winter months, the average bee colony eats about 50 pounds of honey! In February, the queen bee mates with male bees called drones. Then she starts laying eggs. She may lay as many as 1,500 eggs in a day! This is tiring for her. She has 12 bees to guard, clean, and feed her.

In late March, female bees called workers leave the hive to search for flowers. In northern areas they may have to wait until April to find any flowers. The field worker bees spend many hours each day gathering nectar and pollen from spring flowers, especially cherry blossoms. The bees then change the nectar into honey and store the pollen to eat for protein.

Each May, a new queen is born. The old queen and about half of the worker bees leave the hive and fly away in a swarm. They build a new hive and start a new colony. Queens live about four years. All other bees live 6 weeks (drones) or 16 weeks (workers). The hive worker bees are responsible for feeding the baby bees a mixture of honey and pollen called beebread. The drones hang around the hive and don't even feed themselves. The worker bees do everything for them.

Bees make more honey in July, August, and September than in all of the other months of the year. In late summer the worker bees use bee glue to mend cracks around the cells where new bees are developing. These same bees store honey around the cells, too. Workers use beeswax to make honeycomb. They gather and store all the honey and pollen. They also care for the baby bees and drones and guard the hive. It's no wonder they're called workers!

In September, the worker bees spend every daylight moment visiting as many flowers as possible. A bee may stop at 600 flowers in one day! At the end of this month, the drones fly away and die, since they are no longer needed. Keeping them alive would take too much honey. New drones will be born for the next mating season. Instinct tells a bee to leave the hive when it is going to die. This keeps the hive free of dead bodies.

In October, workers bring back water and plant sap. They use these things to seal the hive against bad weather. The queen stops laying eggs in the winter. These last eggs will grow into the drones for her next mating season. As the weather grows colder, the worker bees gather closely around their queen. They rapidly move their wings to keep her warm.

Writing

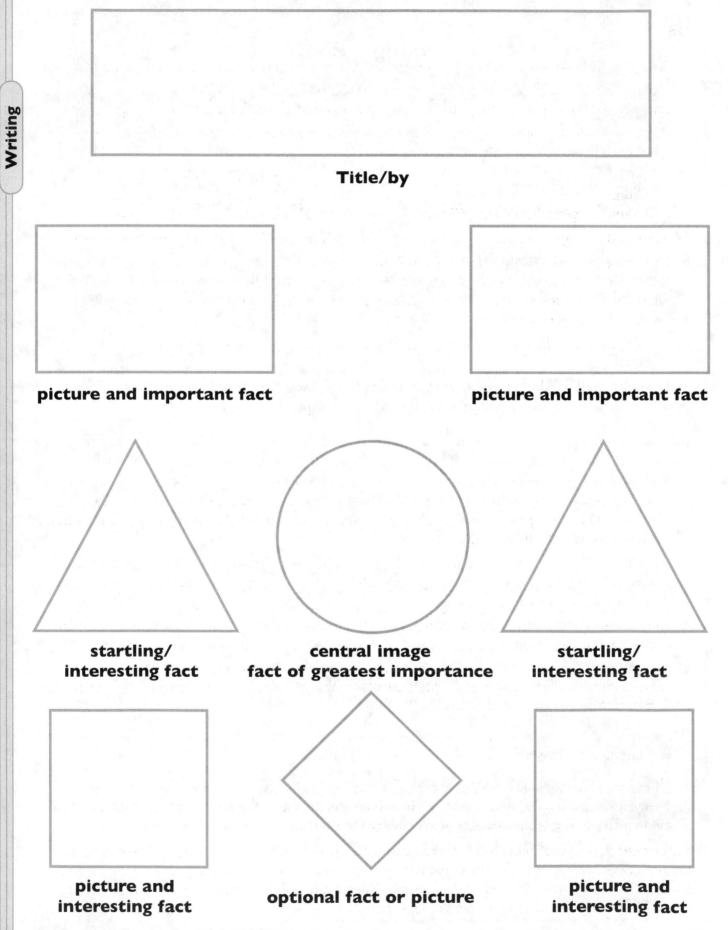

Title/by

picture and important fact

picture and important fact

**startling/
interesting fact**

**central image
fact of greatest importance**

**startling/
interesting fact**

**picture and
interesting fact**

optional fact or picture

**picture and
interesting fact**

Day 1

1. Ask your students what a prefix is. See if they can name a few examples. List them on the board. Ask for words that have each listed prefix and write those words, too.

2. Explain that your students are going to study the prefix *un-*, which means "not."

3. Ask your students what a suffix is and ask for some examples. List them on the board. Ask for words that have each suffix and list them, too.

4. Introduce the suffix *-ly*. Adding *-ly* to the end of a word turns it into an adverb. Write the definition of an adverb on the board. (*An adverb modifies, or explains, a verb. It tells how something happens/happened/will happen. An adverb can also modify an adjective.*)

5. Make and display an overhead transparency of the "Ice-Cream Cone" graphic organizer on page 72.

6. One at a time, write the examples given on the completed graphic organizer on page 71. Show the students how to put the word parts together to form a word, and write it on the line. Discuss the meaning of each word and how you know that meaning from its parts. Point out and discuss when *y* should be changed to an *i* before the *-ly* is added.

7. Ask for student volunteers to generate sentences for each of the words. Write them on a blank transparency.

8. Have the students choose two of the words just learned and write a sentence for each. Collect these papers to check for understanding.

Day 2

1. Write these words in parts on the "Ice-Cream Cone" graphic organizer: *un-fair-ly, un-steady-ly, un-expected-ly,* and *un-happy-ly.* You may want to put a star next to the ice-cream scoop for *unsteadily* and *unhappily* to give students the hint that they should change the *y* to *i*. Then make copies and distribute them to the students.

2. Have the students join the word parts on the parts of the ice-cream cone to form the complete words and write them in the place provided. The students then write the meaning of each based on the word parts (no dictionary use).

3. Have the students write a sentence for each of the words on the back of the paper. Collect and check for understanding.

4. Make student copies of "Working with Words" on page 70. Do the first two with the class. (*1. unlikely, 2. unfortunately*) Have the students complete the page for homework. (*3. unnaturally, 4. unsightly, 5. uneasily, 6. unfriendly*)

Day 3

1. Have students exchange papers and correct the homework.

2. Discuss the meaning of each of the words on the graphic organizer the students completed. Read aloud a few of the best sentences generated by the students.

Extension: Give your students a list of adjectives: *common, kind, usual, certain*. Have them add the prefix *un-* and write a silly story that uses each word at least once. Give your students another list of adjectives: *beautiful, soft, noisy, sleepy*. Have them add the suffix *-ly* to the end of each and write a silly story that uses each word at least once.

Working with Words

- The prefix *un-* means "not."

- The suffix *-ly* turns an adjective into an adverb. Then it can explain, or tell more about, a verb or an adjective.

unnaturally	**uneasily**	**unsightly**
unfortunately	**unlikely**	**unfriendly**

Directions: Choose a word from the box to complete the sentence. Each word is used once.

1. With each passing moment it became more _____ that they could reach the station before the train left.

   _____ means _____

2. She had left her homework in school, and _____ the building was now locked for the holiday weekend.

   _____ means _____

3. It seemed creepy because it was _____ quiet in the forest. Not a single sound could be heard.

   _____ means _____

4. The ugly shed with the peeling paint was _____ and appeared out of place in the well-kept garden.

   _____ means _____

5. The boys tiptoed out from their hiding spot and looked around _____.

   _____ means _____

6. Tom hesitated to ask the man because he was scowling and looked really _____.

   _____ means _____

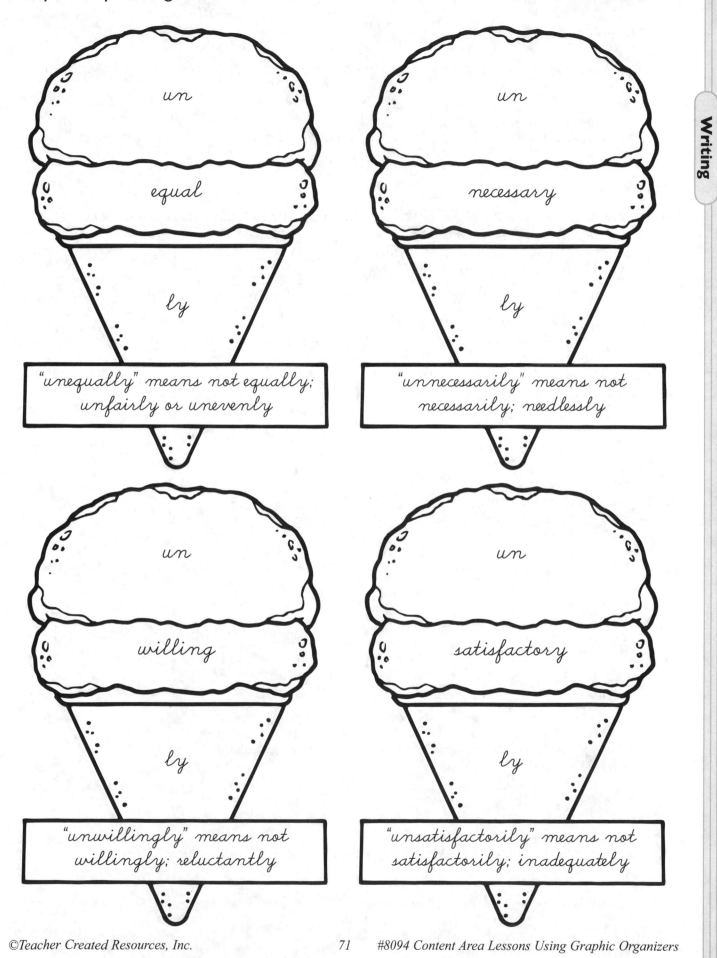

un

equal

ly

"unequally" means not equally; unfairly or unevenly

un

necessary

ly

"unnecessarily" means not necessarily; needlessly

un

willing

ly

"unwillingly" means not willingly; reluctantly

un

satisfactory

ly

"unsatisfactorily" means not satisfactorily; inadequately

Writing

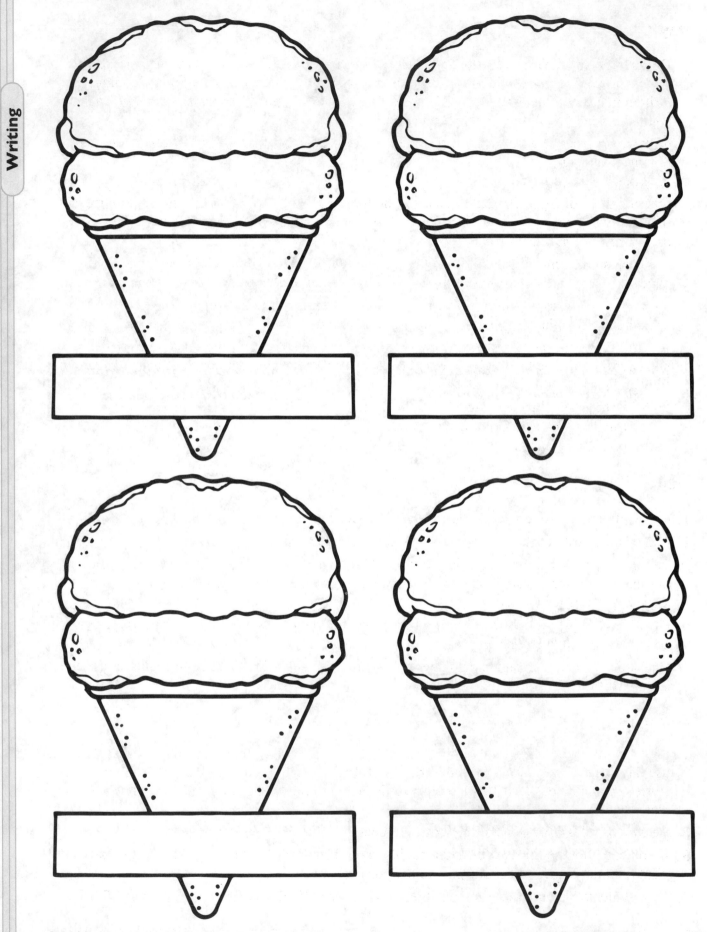

Day 1

1. Define a personal narrative (*a written account in which the central character is the writer; its almost always written in the first-person voice*). Ask your students, "What kinds of things are written in a personal narrative style?" (*Possible answers: diaries, journals, personal letters, emails to friends, autobiographies, anecdotal notes, etc.*)

2. Make an overhead transparency and student copies of the "How It All Fits Together" graphic organizer on page 76.

3. Distribute the copies and display the overhead. Ask your students what the graphic organizer reminds them of (*jigsaw puzzle*). Discuss the four "puzzle pieces" that fit together to form a personal narrative (*"characters" includes "self" and other(s); "highlight" is the main idea the author of the narrative is trying to convey; etc.*).

4. For each student make and distribute three copies of "A Funny Thing Happened to Me" on page 74. Explain that humorous stories are often written in personal narrative form.

5. As a class, read the first story. Decide on the setting, characters, and main highlight (which is always the punchline in a humorous story). Record these on the organizer.

6. Identify the events and list them on the organizer. This step is very important since students' narratives at this age tend to leave out events and details. When that happens, their writing lacks flow and clarity.

7. Pair the students. Have the partners read the second story and fill out the second copy of the "How It All Fits Together" graphic organizer.

8. For homework, each student must fill in the final graphic organizer for the third story.

Day 2

1. Collect the homework assignment to check for understanding.

2. Make and distribute student copies of the graphic organizer.

3. Tell the students that they are going to write their own humorous personal narratives. They have outlined three stories using the graphic organizer. Now they are going to fill it in for their own story in preparation for writing it.

4. Give them a few minutes to think of a funny event in their lives. Then have them independently complete the graphic organizer.

5. Check each student's graphic organizer to be sure he or she included enough events so that the story will flow.

Day 3

1. Students take the information on their graphic organizers and compose their narratives. They can use the title "A Funny Thing Happened to Me" or create a more original one of their own. Their stories should be between 100 and 200 words in length (all of the stories that they analyzed are in that range).

2. Be sure to follow the steps of the writing process.

3. If you can allot the time, let the students illustrate their stories. These would be great pieces to display in the hall for other students to read or for open house.

4. Your students may use these compositions again in the "Word Choice" lesson on pages 77–80.

A Funny Thing Happened to Me

Goosters

One afternoon I taught my four-year-old sister all the different kinds of farm animals in a picture book. When Daddy came home, she was eager to show him that she knew the name of every animal in the book. Flustered and excited, she turned to the bird page and pointed at the picture of the rooster. It was next to the goose. She said, "And this is a gooster."

Daddy is good natured. He laughed and said, "My goodness, I've never heard of a gooster before." My sister gave me a look that meant she thought our dad was dense. But then she smiled at him and said, in a tone that sounded just like a parent, "Don't feel bad! It's just that I've never read you this book before!"

Mumbling Mix-Up

I went with my mom on Take Your Kid to Work Day. She's the manager of a large grocery store. The store employees that give away samples and demonstrate products are called "demo ladies." I was standing near my mom while she was talking to an employee. A woman came up and asked where she could find salsa. Before my mom could speak, I said, "I know! See that demo lady? She's standing at the end of aisle 11. You'll find it there about halfway down on your right."

The customer thanked me and left. Then she returned a few minutes later and said, "Young man, what you said really bothered me. The woman giving out samples at the end of that aisle is not dumb or old!"

I looked at her in shock. I had no idea what she was talking about. She continued, "I want to know why you called her a dumb old lady!" I burst out laughing and couldn't stop. The customer looked really annoyed. My mom came to my rescue by telling her what I'd really said. The lady blushed, said, "Sorry!" and hurried away.

Delicious Side Dish

When I was about six years old, my mom asked me to call Grandma and invite her over for dinner one night. I called and asked Grandma if she'd like to come. To tease me, Grandma said, "Well, now, that depends on what you're having."

I took her seriously. I put down the phone to go see what Mom was making. I rushed back to the phone and said that we were having ham and old, rotten potatoes.

Grandma said, "Really? Old, rotten potatoes?"

I said, "Why, don't you like them?" I was disappointed, thinking that she wouldn't come.

Grandma chuckled and said, "Nobody I know likes to eat old, rotten potatoes. But I'm pretty sure your mom is making au gratin potatoes. I'll see you in half an hour."

Note: This example is filled in with the answers for the third story, which the students do as homework.

Writing

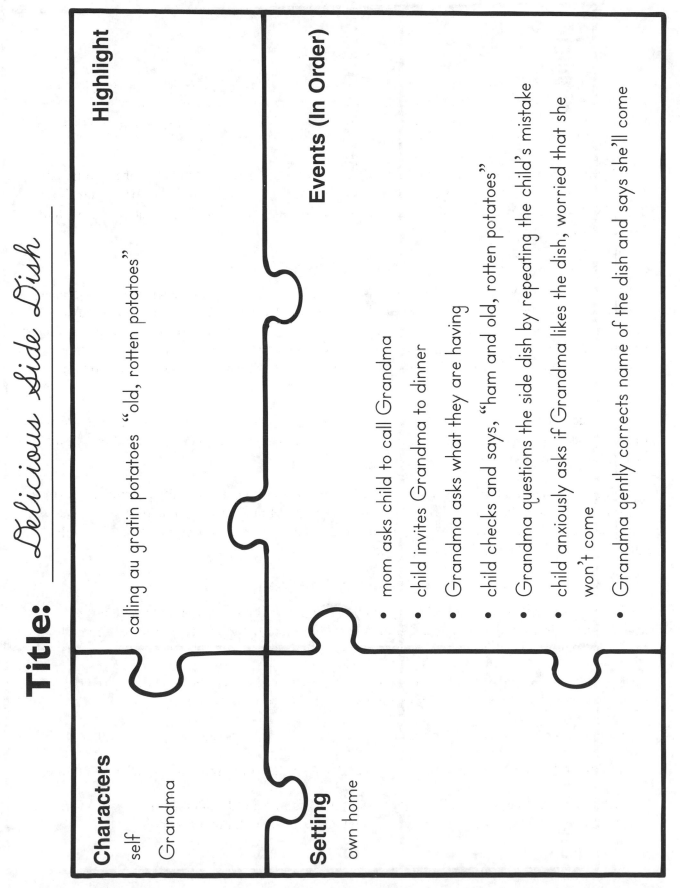

Title: *Delicious Side Dish*

Characters

self

Grandma

Setting

own home

Highlight

calling au gratin potatoes "old, rotten potatoes"

Events (In Order)

- mom asks child to call Grandma
- child invites Grandma to dinner
- Grandma asks what they are having
- child checks and says, "ham and old, rotten potatoes"
- Grandma questions the side dish by repeating the child's mistake
- child anxiously asks if Grandma likes the dish, worried that she won't come
- Grandma gently corrects name of the dish and says she'll come

Writing

Title:

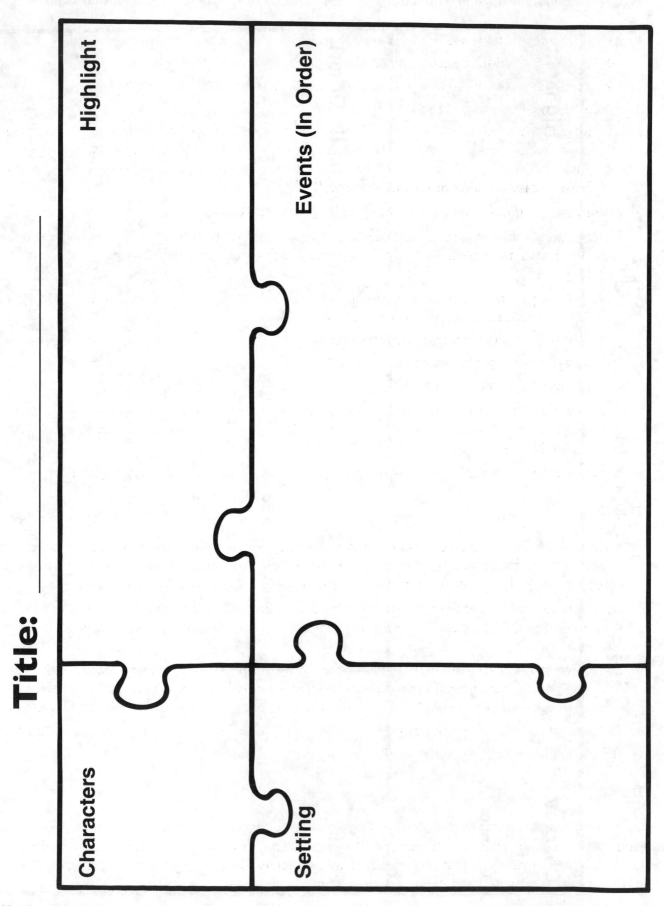

Highlight

Events (In Order)

Characters

Setting

Writing

Day 1

1. Ask your students to define these parts of speech and give you examples for each:
   - ✧ **noun**—a word for a person, place, thing, or concept
   - ✧ **verb**—an action word or one that shows existence (*to be* and its variants)
   - ✧ **adjective**—a word used to describe a noun
   - ✧ **adverb**—a word used to describe a verb, adjective, or another adverb; often ends in -*ly* and answer one of these questions: when?, how?, or how much? Be sure to point out to your students that many adjectives can be made into adverbs with the addition of -*ly* (e.g., noisy—noisily; easy—easily; beautiful—beautifully).

2. Record the definitions and examples on the board or overhead.

3. Make an overhead transparency and student copies of the "Parts of Speech" graphic organizer on page 80. Have the students write the definition of each part of speech below the letters for that part of speech.

4. Make and display an overhead transparency of "The Solitary Owl," an American-Indian myth, on page 78. Introduce any unfamiliar vocabulary:
   - ✧ **solitary**—living alone; without companions
   - ✧ **haughty**—too proud, arrogant
   - ✧ **offended**—angered, upset

5. Tell your class that myths often explain something that happens in nature. As a whole class, read "The Solitary Owl." For each blank, ask your students what part of speech is missing and write it beneath the blank.

6. Reread the myth, asking students to suggest appropriate words for each part of speech.

Day 2

1. Your students can use the personal narratives that they wrote for the lesson on page 73 or let them select another composition from their writing portfolios. Your students are going to revisit their compositions and improve them by making and/or adding appropriate word choices.

2. Have the students reread their pieces. Display these questions on the board or overhead: "Are the nouns used the best ones? How about the verbs? What adjectives could be added? What adverbs?"

3. Have your students take out their copies of the "Parts of Speech" graphic organizer. On it they will jot down the new nouns, verbs, adjectives, and adverbs that they plan to use to make their writing more vivid. They should make at least two changes or additions for each part of speech.

4. The students rewrite their compositions using/adding the new nouns, verbs, adjectives, and adverbs.

5. Have them submit their graphic organizers and the new compositions to you.

Day 3

Ask two or three volunteers to read their pieces aloud. Ask the class members to jot down the adjectives and adverbs on a sheet of paper as they hear them. Discuss these words after each piece is read. You want to make sure that your students are accurately identifying adjectives and adverbs, so this is your opportunity to correct any misconceptions.

Writing

The Solitary Owl

Long ago, all the birds lived together. One day they found a _____ tiger lily. It was the _____ flower any of them had ever seen. Each bird wanted the tiger lily for itself. So they _____ to give it as a prize to the most beautiful bird of all. The birds called together a rabbit, a woodchuck, and a _____. They asked them to act as judges to determine which _____ deserved the _____ flower.

One by one, each of the birds of the world strutted and _____ before the judges. The judges looked at _____ colored cardinals, blue jays, and canaries. They saw snow-white doves, and gleaming black ravens. They looked at falcons, eagles, ducks, pheasants, finches, hummingbirds, and many, many more. The judges found it _____ difficult to choose among so many birds.

Then an owl came forward. "Let me save you some trouble," he said in a haughty _____ . "I am the most beautiful bird. Give me the _____."

The other birds were _____ offended. They _____ , "The only thing that is obvious is that you are not the most beautiful bird. Now the sun is setting. Let's all go _____ and let the judges _____ what they have seen today. Tomorrow _____ they can decide who will _____ the tiger lily."

That night the owl _____ on a tree branch. "If they won't give me the prize, then I shall take it for myself," the owl _____ . In the _____ hour of the night, he _____ flew to the tiger lily, plucked it, and _____ it home.

The next morning the other birds were very angry when they discovered what had happened.

"We must punish that _____ owl," said the robin.

"The _____ stole the tiger lily at night. So he should never fly in daylight again," said the finch.

"He shall see by night but not by day," added the _____ .

"Since he _____ he is so much better than we are, he cannot live with us anymore," said the sparrow.

"So be it," said the eagle.

And that is how the owl became a solitary bird of the night that hides his face all day and flies only under the cover of darkness.

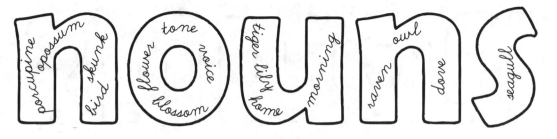

a word for a picture, place, thing, or concept

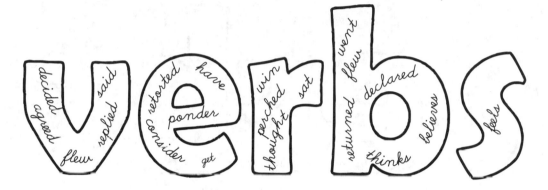

an action word or one that shows existence ("to be" and its variants)

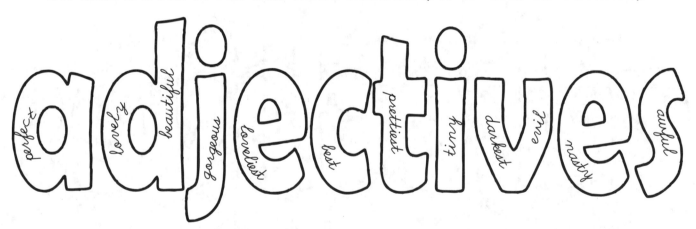

a word used to describe a noun

a word used to describe a verb, adjective, or another adverb

Writing

nouns

verbs

adjectives

adverbs

1. Discuss the importance of visualizing while reading. Making mental images in your mind is one of the best ways to enjoy and understand text, as well as remember what you've read. Ask your students to close their eyes and keep them closed during this guided visualization exercise. Read the sentence in italics, then ask the questions. The students are to answer the questions in their minds, not aloud.

   • *Once upon a time long, long ago, a cottage stood in a clearing of a deep, dark, forest.*

   "Picture the cottage in your mind. What is it made of—bricks, cobblestones, wood? What's the roof made of? Is the cottage pretty? old? falling down? Does it have windows? How many?"

   • *Inside the cottage lived a family of trolls.*

   "Look at the trolls. How many are there? What do they look like? How tall are they? Do they have hair? What color is it? What color eyes do they have? What color is their skin? Are all the trolls the same size? Do they look alike? Does knowing that trolls live inside change your image of the cottage?"

2. Have the students open their eyes and discuss what they visualized. Explain that everyone's ideas are correct. However, they must be willing to change their images as the story or poem gives more details.

3. Make student copies of "Mr. Nobody" on page 82. Introduce any unfamiliar vocabulary:

   ✧ **'tis**—archaic contraction for "it is"

   ✧ **ajar**—slightly open (as with a door)

   ✧ **afar**—great distance away

   ✧ **prithee** (PRITH-ee)—archaic word meaning "please"

   ✧ **'round**—abbreviation of "around" to make it one syllable

4. Read the poem aloud to your class as the students follow along. Then, reread it chorally.

5. Ask your class, "Which thing that Mr. Nobody was blamed for is impossible to visualize?" (*not oiling the squeaky door*) Then ask, "Why is it impossible to visualize Mr. Nobody?" (*because he does not exist—he's an imaginary character whom the author blames for all his or her own misdeeds*)

6. Write this question on the board: "Picture the results of Mr. Nobody's naughty deeds. Which ones create the strongest mental pictures?" Have your students read the poem again silently to themselves to answer this question.

7. Make an overhead transparency and student copies of the "Photo Album" graphic organizer on page 84.

8. Display the transparency. Read the first stanza. Draw a picture of a cracked plate on the transparency in the first photo slot. Write as its caption: "Mr. Nobody cracks plates."

9. Distribute the student copies of the graphic organizer. Ask the students to identify their four most vivid images of the results of Mr. Nobody's bad deeds. They are to draw and label them in the photo album slots on the graphic organizer.

10. Collect the completed graphic organizers and check for understanding.

Mr. Nobody

I know a funny little man who's as quiet as a mouse,

Who does the mischief that is done in everybody's house!

There's no one ever sees his face, and yet we all agree

That every plate we break was cracked by Mr. Nobody.

'Tis he who always tears our books, who leaves the door ajar,

He pulls the buttons from our shirts and scatters pins afar.

That squeaking door will always squeak, for prithee, don't you see,

We leave the oiling to be done by Mr. Nobody.

The fingerprints upon the door by none of us are made;

We never leave the blinds unclosed to let the curtains fade.

The milk we never spill; the boots that lying 'round you see

Are not our boots—they all belong to Mr. Nobody.

Directions: Draw the four "snapshots" that the words let you form in your mind.

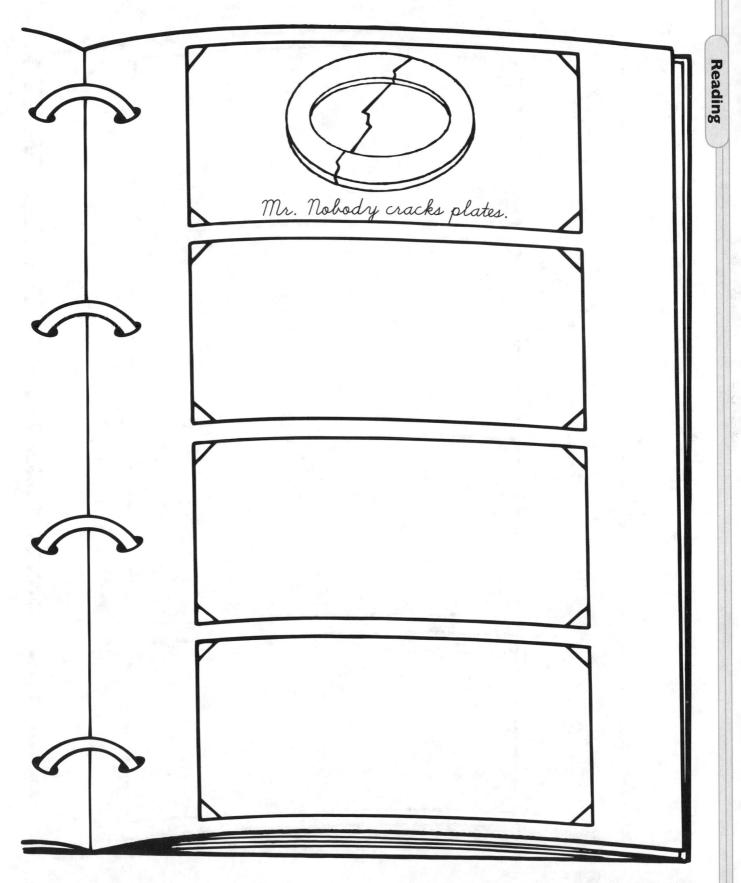

Mr. Nobody cracks plates.

Blank Graphic Organizer

Photo Album

Directions: Draw the four "snapshots" that the words let you form in your mind.

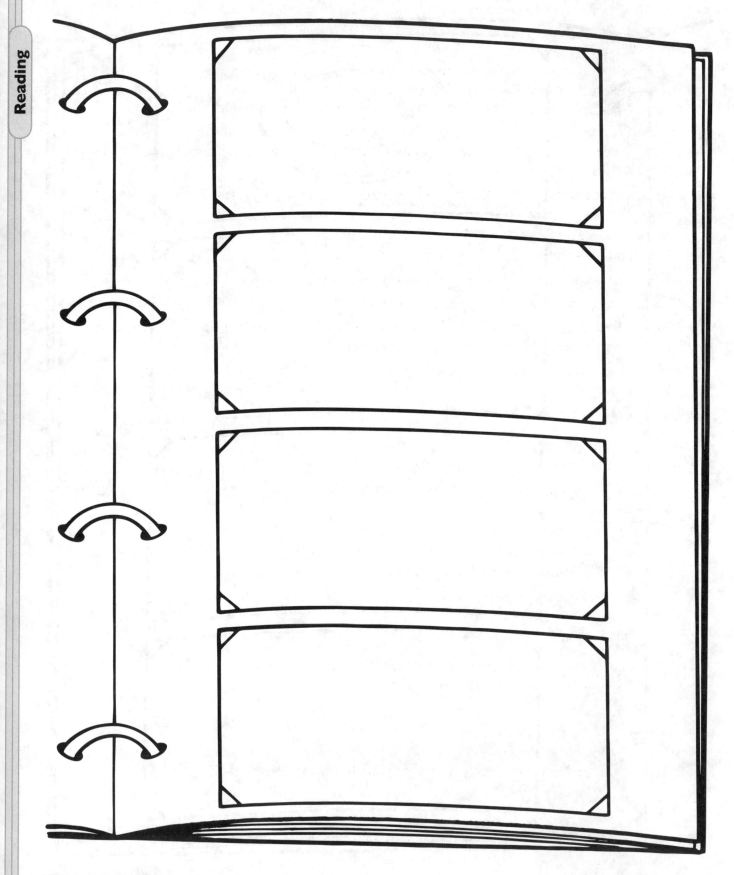

Day 1

1. This lesson teaches your students to read and understand a fable, which is a story with a moral. A fable is a type of allegory. An allegory is a story in which its characters or action are meant to represent something else.

2. Introduce the word *fable* and have students tell you what they already know about the topic. See if any student can relate a famous fable (such as the fox and the "sour" grapes or the dog who dropped his piece of meat in the stream for the "bigger one" in the water's reflection).

3. Discuss Aesop, a slave in ancient Greece who collected stories from travelers from around the world. Since he could write, he recorded these stories. His fables are probably the best-known, but his stories originated in Africa, Europe, and Asia.

4. Make student copies of "The 'Sick' Lion" on page 86. Introduce any unfamiliar vocabulary:
   - ❖ **hyena**—a dog-like African mammal that lives on the savanna (plains)
   - ❖ **negligence**—lack of proper care and attention
   - ❖ **harmless**—unable to do harm or injury

5. Distribute the copies and have the students read the fable. It is written at a 4.3 reading level.

6. Make an overhead transparency and student copies of the graphic organizer on page 88.

7. Display the transparency and distribute the student copies. Ask the students to volunteer the answers to title, setting (*around the lion's cave*), and characters (*Lion, Hyena,* and *Fox*).

8. Remove the "Story Outline" transparency and put a plain transparency on the overhead. Have your students take turns listing the events that occurred in order. Based on the list of events, challenge your students to come up with a brief (no more than two sentences) but descriptive beginning. This is a great sentence-building opportunity. Show them how to pack a lot of information into a one- or two-sentence summary. Repeat this step for the middle and end, as well. The emphasis is on concise accuracy.

9. As you transfer the information to the graphic organizer transparency, have students do so on their own organizers.

10. Discuss the moral for the story. There are two standard "morals" given for this fable:
    - Just because everyone else is doing it, that doesn't make it a smart thing to do.
    - Don't just follow the crowd; think for yourself.

11. Accept a moral that meets either of these standards, regardless of its wording.

Days 2–3

Distribue new copies of the graphic organizer. Pair your students and ask them to create a fable. Give them time to write it and edit it.

Day 4

Have students fold under the part that tells their fable's morals and exchange fables with other pairs. See if the students can generate the morals for their classmates' fables.

Day 5

Choose three of the students' fables to read aloud to the whole group. Discuss the morals that the students have assigned to them. Does the class agree?

The "Sick" Lion

One day the lion, king of all the beasts, did not come out of his cave. Instead, he lay groaning and murmuring faint roars whenever anyone came near.

The other animals did not know what to do. For as long as they could remember, the lion had made all their decisions. They had long since forgotten how to think for themselves. After much discussion they agreed that they must visit him in his cave. If they stayed away he would be angry, and they would suffer once he got well. Besides, in his current condition he couldn't harm them.

So, one at a time, the animals went into the royal cave. Some took him a gift, such as the best bit of meat from a recent catch. Others just went to ask about his health. Large and small, each animal in the lion's kingdom made its way to his home.

However, the fox stayed away. After a time, the lion noticed that the fox never visited. So he sent his servant, a hyena, to ask why the fox was being so rude.

"Fox," said the hyena, "you have displeased His Majesty the lion. Although he is ill, you have not even put your nose inside his cave to ask how he is feeling. What excuse do you have for your negligence?"

The clever fox replied, "Hyena, I would like to see the king, for I respect him. Indeed, I went to the mouth of the cave with my best piece of meat as a get-well present."

"And?" the hyena prompted.

"Although I wanted to see the king, when I got there I saw something that made me too afraid to go in," said the fox.

"And what was that?" asked the hyena.

The fox replied, "I saw footprints in the sand from all sorts of animals. But they were all going one way—into the cave. Not a single footprint came out. I did not want to enter a place from which I would never return."

The clever fox had figured out the lion's evil plan. Thinking he was sick and harmless, the animals he usually had to chase for food were all coming right into his cave—and ending up as his next meal.

Title: The "Sick" Lion

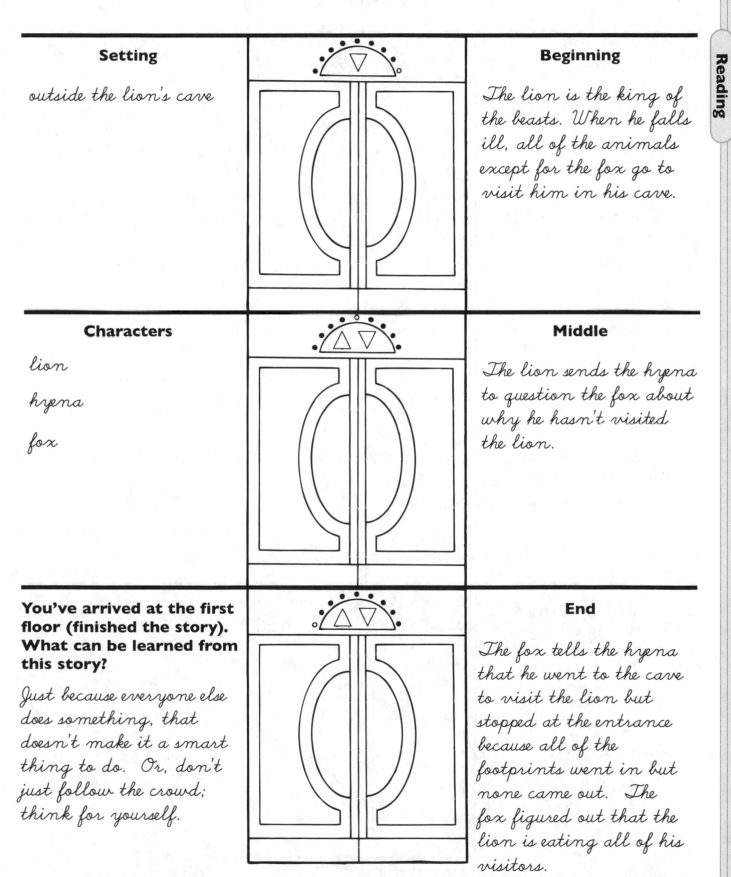

Setting

outside the lion's cave

Beginning

The lion is the king of the beasts. When he falls ill, all of the animals except for the fox go to visit him in his cave.

Characters

lion

hyena

fox

Middle

The lion sends the hyena to question the fox about why he hasn't visited the lion.

You've arrived at the first floor (finished the story). What can be learned from this story?

Just because everyone else does something, that doesn't make it a smart thing to do. Or, don't just follow the crowd; think for yourself.

End

The fox tells the hyena that he went to the cave to visit the lion but stopped at the entrance because all of the footprints went in but none came out. The fox figured out that the lion is eating all of his visitors.

Reading

Title: _____

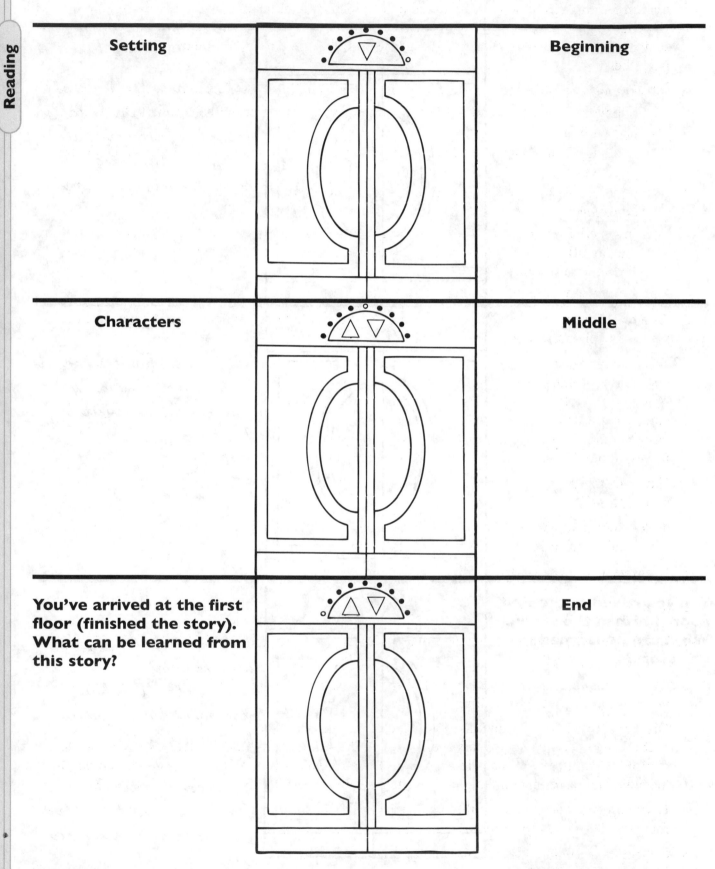

Setting

Beginning

Characters

Middle

You've arrived at the first floor (finished the story). What can be learned from this story?

End

Day 1

1. Learning to figure out new words based on context is a vital reading skill that allows your students to read independently with confidence while building their vocabulary. Write these sentences on the board to illustrate the six types of context clues. Omit the information in parentheses:

   1. The <u>unkempt</u> boy wore a torn, stained T-shirt. (*definition given by other words or phrases*)
   2. Sue was very overweight, but her <u>obesity</u> never bothered her until she went to high school. (*synonym*)
   3. Although Benito had saved his money for months in order to go to the concert, the ticket price was too <u>exorbitant</u>. (*contrast*)
   4. Tundra, desert, grassland, and rain forest are the names of four of Earth's <u>biomes</u>. (*summary*)
   5. In America, the end of World War II was marked by <u>euphoria</u>. Businesses gave workers the day off with pay. People sang and danced in the streets. Nearly every large city held fireworks or a parade. (*mood*)
   6. Her voice was so <u>shrill</u> that it hurt my ears. (*logic*)

2. As a class, determine the meaning of each word you underlined. Whenever possible, have the students explain the process they used to figure out the meaning.

3. The clue type is given in parentheses after each sentence. Label each one on the board and discuss its meaning. For the first one, the definition was given elsewhere. In the second, a synonym provided the clue. The third sentence relies on contrast; the meaning is implied by comparing it with a known word or concept. In the fourth, the word sums up a list. The fifth is based on mood, as the meaning is implied by information from the larger context. The sixth one involves logic; based on the information given, a person can surmise what the word must mean.

4. Have your students add these sentences and the type of context clues they show to a journal or notebook.

5. Make student copies of "The Optimist" on pages 90–91. Do not preview the story or introduce any vocabulary. It is written at a 2.9 reading level.

6. Reconvene as a class. Briefly discuss the story.

Day 2

1. Make an overhead transparency and two copies for each student of the "Root Beer Float" graphic organizer on page 93.

2. Direct your students' attention to the boldface words in "The Optimist." These are the new vocabulary words that they figured out using context.

3. Display the transparency and distribute one of the student copies. As a class, fill it in for the first four words. The vocabulary word goes on the straw. The students' definition (do not use a dictionary) for that word goes in the foam. Have the students describe how they figured out the meaning and write that on the glass. Write the type of context clue used below the glass.

4. Distribute the second copy of the organizer. Have students independently complete it for the last four boldface words (*prosperous, incredulous, furious, stunned*).

5. Collect the graphic organizers to check for understanding.

The Optimist

There once was a woman named Hilda. She was an **optimist** who saw something good in every situation. She lived with her husband Morris. They were poor, but when they could, they saved coins in a jar. After years, Hilda said, "Morris, at last we have enough to buy a cow. It would be great to have milk and cheese and butter! Please buy us a cow."

So Morris walked to the market many miles away and bought a cow. It took every single cent in the jar. As Morris led the cow home, he met a woman with a pig. She said, "That's a fine-looking cow, sir. Will you trade it for my pig?"

Morris said, "Say! Then we could have bacon! Yes, I'll trade."

A little later, a man came down the road with a goat. He said, "That's a nice pig. Would you trade it for my goat?"

Morris thought to himself that a goat was even better than a pig. They could have milk and cheese and when it died, meat. So he traded the pig for the goat. Then he stopped in a meadow to let his goat **graze**. A shepherd leading his flock through the field said, "Hey! I've been looking for a sturdy goat. Would you trade your goat for the largest sheep in my flock?"

Morris said, "I bet Hilda would like to have wool to make some new clothes! Yes, I'll trade." When Morris was about halfway home, he met a woman with a hen. She pleaded with him to trade his ram for it. She said that she had six children without clothing for the coming winter. Morris knew that Hilda wouldn't want children to be without warm clothing. And the hen would give eggs for years and when it died, meat. So even though it was an awful deal, he traded the goat for the hen.

Now a cold wind began to blow. Morris shivered and feared that his fingers would get **frostbite**. Then he spied a man selling gloves. Morris told him, "I have no money, but I will give you my hen for a pair of gloves."

The **astonished** glove salesman said, "You would give a *hen* for *gloves*?!"

Morris responded, "Better to keep my fingers than the hen." So they made the trade.

Morris was close to home when he met a **prosperous** man named Sherwin. He told Morris that he was lonely and asked him to keep him company.

Morris said, "I'll tell you about my day. I took our life savings to market to buy a cow.

Sherwin asked, "Then where's the cow?"

Morris said, "Oh, I traded her for a pig on the way home."

"Then where's the pig?"

"I traded it for a goat."

"Then where's the goat?"

"I traded it for a sheep."

Sherwin cried, "But you have no sheep!"

Morris replied, "That's because I traded it for a hen."

Sherwin looked **incredulous**. "Why did you do that? That's a horrible trade!"

Morris explained, "Then I traded the hen for these gloves to save my hands from frostbite."

The Optimist *(cont.)*

Sherwin said, "What?! You took your life savings to market, and you're returning with a pair of gloves? Your wife will be **furious**! I wouldn't want to be in your shoes."

Morris smiled and said, "Hilda won't be upset. She is an optimist."

Sherwin said, "You have got to be kidding me."

Morris responded, "She won't say one cross word when I tell her about today's events."

Sherwin said, "I am wealthy, so if what you say is true, I'll give you a $100 bill."

Morris was thrilled. One hundred dollars was more than the cow had cost! He said, "Sherwin, stand just outside my door and listen."

Then Morris entered the house saying, "Hilda, I'm home!"

Hilda greeted him with a hug. She cried, " I was getting worried about you. It's grown so cold and windy!"

Morris smiled, "I hope you've got supper ready, for I've walked many miles today without eating."

Hilda put a plate in front of Morris, saying, "Tell me about your day."

Morris said, "I found a good cow and bought her."

Hilda said, "Wonderful! I'll take care of our cow after I finish eating."

Morris said, "I don't have the cow. I traded her for a pig."

Hilda cried, "How clever! Now we'll have bacon. A cow might eat more hay than we could provide. I'll take care of our pig after I finish eating."

Morris said, "I don't have the pig. I traded it for a goat."

Hilda smiled. "That's great! After all, we'd eat the pig and then have nothing left. With a goat we'll have milk and cheese and then meat when it dies. I'll take care of our goat after I finish eating."

Morris said, "I don't have the goat. I traded it for a sheep so you could have wool to make yourself clothes."

Hilda said, "How thoughtful! I'll take care of our sheep after I finish eating."

"I don't have the sheep. I traded it for a hen. A woman said she needed the sheep's wool to make clothing for her six children."

Hilda nodded. "That's just what I would have done! After all, I have no spinning wheel. Now I won't have to make new clothes. I can get along fine with what I have. I'll take care of our hen after I finish eating."

"I no longer have the hen. It was so cold on the way home that my fingers nearly froze. I gave the hen to a man for a pair of gloves."

Hilda looked **stunned**. Then she said, "Morris, I'm so glad that you don't have frostbite! Why would I need a cow, or a pig, or a goat, or a sheep, or a hen? You're all I need to be happy!"

Morris got up and went to the front door. Sherwin stepped into the house, handed him a $100 bill, and said, "Morris, you earned this $100 fair and square!"

Morris smiled and shook his head. "No, Hilda did by being an optimist."

a person who sees the good in any situation

optimist

"She was an optimist who could find something good in every situation."

definition

eat grass

graze

reason Morris stopped in meadow for goat

logic

damage to body caused by being too cold

frostbite

"a cold wind began to blow fiercely"; Morris had no warm gloves; he was afraid for his fingers

logic

surprised; amazed

astonished

salesman seems shocked that Morris will trade the hen for gloves; Sherwin says it's a horrible trade

mood

Reading

Day 1

1. This lesson works well as a follow-up to the vocabulary in context lesson that begins on page 89. It is recommended that you do that lesson first. However, this lesson can be done independently.

2. Make and distribute student copies of "The Optimist" on pages 90–91.

3. If you have not done the "Vocabulary in Context" lesson, introduce unfamiliar words:
   - **optimist**—person who sees the bright side of any situation
   - **graze**—eat grass
   - **frostbite**—damage to flesh caused by extreme cold
   - **astonished**—amazed, surprised
   - **prosperous**—wealthy, rich, well-to-do
   - **incredulous**—unbelieving; amazed
   - **furious**—angry; very mad
   - **stunned**—shocked

4. Distribute the copies and have your students read the story independently. It is written at a 2.9 reading level.

5. Make an overhead transparency and student copies of the "Storyline" graphic organizer on page 96.

6. Display the transparency and distribute the student copies. Explain that a story's plot is the series of events that make up its storyline. As much as possible, have the students volunteer the information for each part of the graphic organizer. They can abbreviate names when writing on the articles of clothing. They can use "M" for Morris, "H" for Hilda, and "S" for Sherwin. Have students fill in their graphic organizers at their seats while you do so at the overhead.

7. Do not answer the question at the bottom of the graphic organizer.

Day 2

1. Tell your students that when authors write, they want to have an effect on their readers. They want to make their readers think. Authors write for three main purposes: to inform, to entertain, or to persuade. Ask your class, "When you read, how can you tell the author's purpose? What kind of things would indicate that the author wanted to inform? entertain? persuade?"

2. Have your students get out their "Storyline" graphic organizers from yesterday. Then discuss, "Why did the author write 'The Optimist?'" Guide them to understand that even when the author's purpose is to entertain, there is usually an underlying message that the author wants to convey. As a class, decide what to write at the bottom of the graphic organizer.

3. Make new student copies of the "Storyline" graphic organizer.

4. Choose a story from your basal series or find and make student copies of another short story.

5. Depending upon the needs of your class, have your students read the story independently or in pairs. Then have them fill out a new "Storyline" graphic organizer.

6. Collect these graphic organizers and evaluate for understanding.

Title: _The Optimist_

Major Characters: _Morris (M)_

Hilda (H)

Setting: _H and M's house; along the road_
from their home to the town

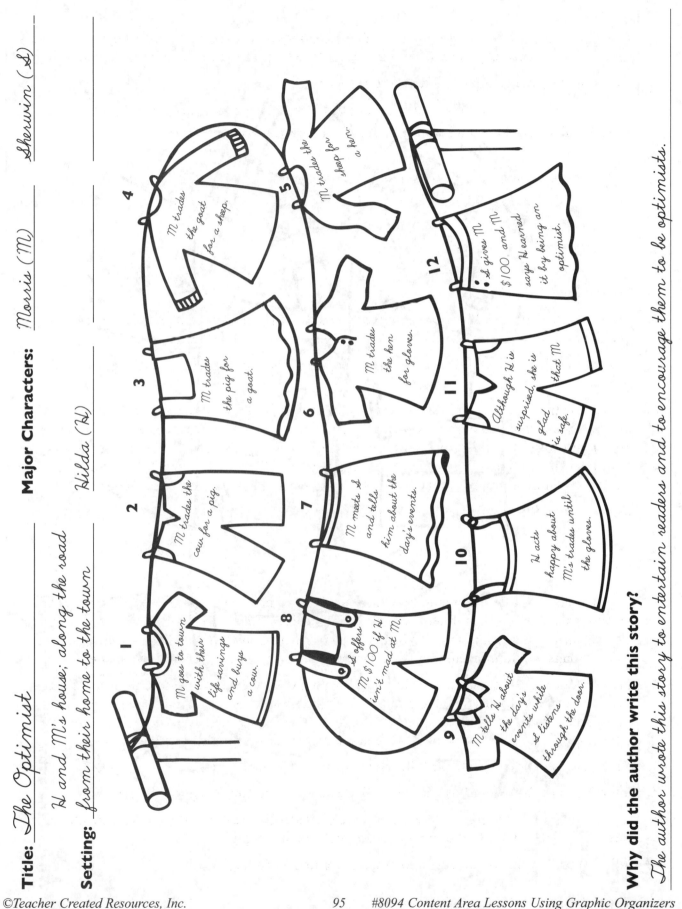

1. _M goes to town with their life savings and buys a cow._

2. _M trades the cow for a pig._

3. _M trades the pig for a goat._

4. _M trades the goat for a sheep._

5. _M trades the sheep for a hen._

6. _M trades the hen for gloves._

7. _M meets L and tells him about the day's events._

8. _L offers M $100 if H isn't mad at M._

9. _M tells H about the day's events while L listens through the door._

10. _H acts happy about M's trades until the gloves._

11. _Although H is surprised, she is glad M is safe._

12. _L gives M $100 and says H learned it by being an optimist._

Why did the author write this story?

The author wrote this story to entertain readers and to encourage them to be optimists.

Blank Graphic Organizer   *Storyline*

Major Characters:

Title: _____

Setting: _____

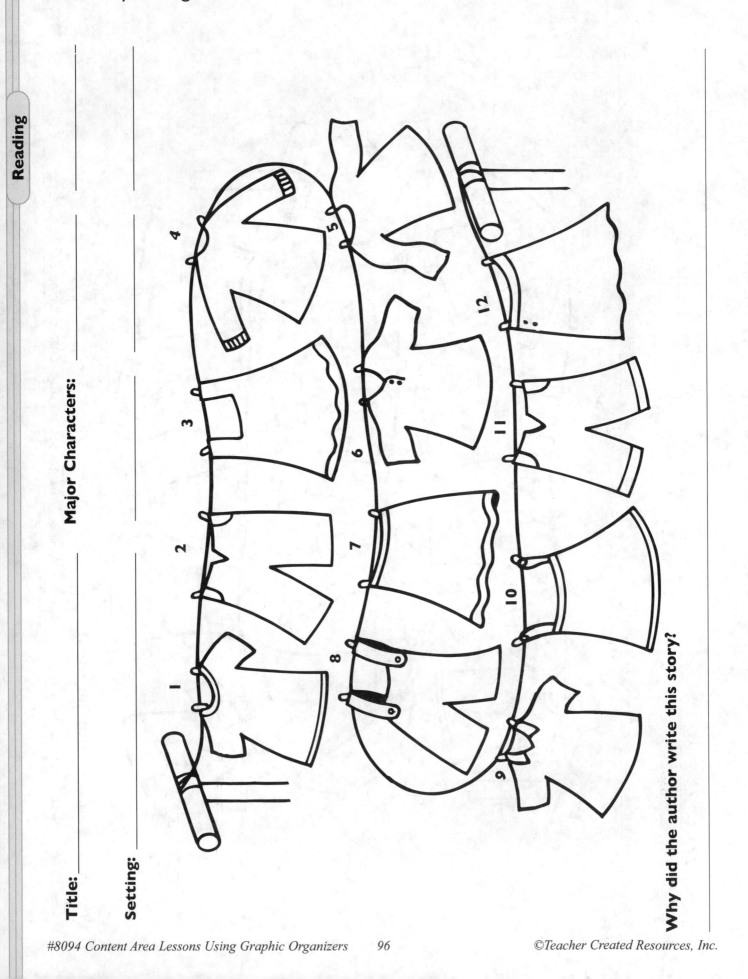

Why did the author write this story?